SILAS MARNER

George Eliot

TECHNICAL DIRECTOR Maxwell Krohn
EDITORIAL DIRECTOR Justin Kestler
MANAGING EDITOR Ben Florman

SERIES EDITORS Boomie Aglietti, Justin Kestler
PRODUCTION Christian Lorentzen

WRITERS Drake P. Bennett, Debra Grossman
EDITORS Matt Blanchard, John Crowther

SPARKNOTES is a registered trademark of SparkNotes LLC.

This edition published by Spark Publishing

Spark Publishing
A Division of SparkNotes LLC
120 Fifth Avenue, 8th Floor
New York, NY 10011

02 03 04 05 SN 9 8 7 6 5 4 3 2 1

Please send all comments and questions or report errors to
feedback@sparknotes.com.

Library of Congress information available upon request

Printed and bound in the United States

RRD-C

ISBN 1-58663-438-0

INTRODUCTION: STOPPING TO BUY SPARKNOTES ON A SNOWY EVENING

Whose words these are you *think* you know.
Your paper's due tomorrow, though;
We're glad to see you stopping here
To get some help before you go.

Lost your course? You'll find it here.
Face tests and essays without fear.
Between the words, good grades at stake:
Get great results throughout the year.

Once school bells caused your heart to quake
As teachers circled each mistake.
Use SparkNotes and no longer weep,
Ace every single test you take.

Yes, books are lovely, dark, and deep,
But only what you grasp you keep,
With hours to go before you sleep,
With hours to go before you sleep.

CONTENTS

CONTEXT

GEORGE ELIOT WAS THE PSEUDONYM of Mary Ann Evans, born in 1819 at the estate of her father's employer in Chilvers Coton, Warwickshire, England. She was sent to boarding school, where she developed a strong religious faith, deeply influenced by the evangelical preacher Rev. John Edmund Jones. After her mother's death, Evans moved with her father to the city of Coventry. There she met Charles and Caroline Bray, progressive intellectuals who led her to question her faith. In 1842 she stopped going to church, and this renunciation of her faith put a strain on Evans's relationship with her father that did not ease for several years.

Evans became acquainted with intellectuals in Coventry who broadened her mind beyond a provincial perspective. Through her new associations, she traveled to Geneva and then to London, where she worked as a freelance writer. In London she met George Lewes, who became her husband in all but the legal sense—a true legal marriage was impossible, as Lewes already had an estranged wife. At this point in her life Evans was still primarily interested in philosophy, but Lewes persuaded her to turn her hand to fiction instead. The publication of her first collection of stories in 1857, under the male pseudonym of George Eliot, brought immediate acclaim from critics as prestigious as Charles Dickens and William Makepeace Thackeray, as well as much speculation about the identity of the mysterious George Eliot. After the publication of her next book and first novel, *Adam Bede,* a number of impostors claimed authorship. In response, Evans asserted herself as the true author, causing quite a stir in a society that still regarded women as incapable of serious writing. Lewes died in 1878, and in 1880 Evans married a banker named John Walter Cross, who was twenty-one years her junior. She died the same year.

Eliot wrote the novels *Adam Bede* (1859) and *The Mill on the Floss* (1860) before publishing *Silas Marner* (1861), the tale of a lonely, miserly village weaver transformed by the love of his adopted daughter. Eliot is best known, however, for *Middlemarch* (1871–1872). Subtitled "A Study in Provincial Life," this lengthy work tells the story of a small English village and its inhabitants, centering on the idealistic and self-sacrificing Dorothea Brooke.

Eliot's novels are deeply philosophical. In exploring the inner workings of her characters and their relationship to their environment, she drew on influences that included the English poet William Wordsworth, the Italian poet Dante, the English art critic John Ruskin, and the Portuguese-Dutch philosopher Baruch Spinoza, whose work Eliot translated into English. The philosophical concerns and references found in her novels—and the refusal to provide the requisite happy ending—struck some contemporary critics as unbecoming in a lady novelist. Eliot's detailed and insightful psychological portrayals of her characters, as well as her exploration of the complex ways these characters confront moral dilemmas, decisively broke from the plot-driven domestic melodrama that had previously served as the standard for the Victorian novel. Eliot's break from tradition inspired the modern novel and inspired numerous future authors, among them Henry James, who admirered Eliot.

Silas Marner was Eliot's third novel and is among the best known of her works. Many of the novel's themes and concerns stem from Eliot's own life experiences. Silas's loss of religious faith recalls Eliot's own struggle with her faith, and the novel's setting in the vanishing English countryside reflects Eliot's concern that England was fast becoming industrialized and impersonal. The novel's concern with class and family can likewise be linked back to Eliot's own life. The voice of the novel's narrator can thus, to some extent, be seen as Eliot's own voice—one tinged with slight condescension, but fond of the setting and thoroughly empathetic with the characters. Though *Silas Marner* is in a sense a very personal novel for Eliot, its treatment of the themes of faith, family, and class has nonetheless given it universal appeal, especially at the time of publication, when English society and institutions were undergoing rapid change.

THE EPIGRAPH

> *"A child, more than all other gifts*
> *That earth can offer to declining man,*
> *Brings hope with it, and forward-looking thoughts."*
> —William Wordsworth

At his death, eleven years before the publication of *Silas Marner,* William Wordsworth was widely considered the most important English writer of his time. His intensely personal poetry, with its simple language and rhythms, marked a revolutionary departure from the complex, formal structures and classical subject matter of his predecessors, poets such as John Dryden and Alexander Pope. Unlike the poetry of Dryden and Pope, Wordsworth's poems are meditative rather than narrative. They celebrate beauty and simplicity most often most often located in the natural landscape. Wordsworth's influence on English poetry—at a time when poetry was unquestioningly held to be the most important form of literature—was enormous. Along with Samuel Taylor Coleridge, Wordsworth set in motion the Romantic era, inspiring a generation of poets that included John Keats, Percy Bysshe Shelley, and Lord Byron.

George Eliot evidently felt a kinship with Wordsworth and his strong identification with the English landscape. Like Wordsworth, Eliot draws many of her metaphors from the natural world. However, the Wordsworth epigraph she chose for *Silas Marner* also highlights the philosophical aspect of her affinity with Wordsworth. Like Eliot, Wordsworth had tried his hand at philosophy before turning to more literary pursuits, and in his poetry he works out his conception of human consciousness. One of Wordsworth's major ideas, radical at the time, was that at the moment of birth, human beings move from a perfect, idealized "otherworld" to this imperfect world, characterized by injustice and corruption. Children, being closest to that otherworld, can remember its beauty and purity, seeing its traces in the natural world around them. As they grow up, however, they lose that connection and forget the knowledge they had as children. However, as described in the quote Eliot has chosen, children and the memories of childhood they evoke in adults can still bring us close to that early, idyllic state. It is not hard to imagine that Eliot had this model in mind when she wrote her story of a child bringing a man out of isolation and spiritual desolation.

Plot Overview

SILAS MARNER IS THE WEAVER in the English countryside village of Raveloe in the early nineteenth century. Like many weavers of his time, he is an outsider—the object of suspicion because of his special skills and the fact that he has come to Raveloe from elsewhere. The villagers see Silas as especially odd because of the curious cataleptic fits he occasionally suffers. Silas has ended up in Raveloe because the members of his religious sect in Lantern Yard, an insular neighborhood in a larger town, falsely accused him of theft and excommunicated him.

Much shaken after the accusation, Silas finds nothing familiar in Raveloe to reawaken his faith and falls into a numbing routine of solitary work. His one attempt at neighborliness backfires: when an herbal remedy he suggests for a neighbor's illness works, he is rumored to be a sort of witch doctor. With little else to live for, Silas becomes infatuated with the money he earns for his work and hoards it, living off as little as possible. Every night he pulls his gold out from its hiding place beneath his floorboards to count it. He carries on in this way for fifteen years.

Squire Cass is the wealthiest man in Raveloe, and his two eldest sons are Godfrey and Dunstan, or Dunsey. Dunsey is greedy and cruel, and enjoys tormenting Godfrey, the eldest son. Godfrey is good-natured but weak-willed, and, though secretly married to the opium addict Molly Farren, he is in love with Nancy Lammeter. Dunsey talked Godfrey into the marriage and repeatedly blackmails him with threats to reveal the marriage to their father. Godfrey gives Dunsey 100 pounds of the rent money paid to him by one of their father's tenants. Godfrey then finds himself in a bind when Dunsey insists that Godfrey repay the sum himself. Dunsey once again threatens to reveal Godfrey's marriage but, after some arguing, offers to sell Godfrey's prize horse, Wildfire, to repay the loan.

The next day, Dunsey meets with some friends who are hunting and negotiates the sale of the horse. Dunsey decides to participate in the hunt before finalizing the sale, and, in doing so, he has a riding accident that kills the horse. Knowing the rumors of Silas's hoard, Dunsey makes plans to intimidate the weaver into lending him money. His walk home takes him by Silas's cottage, and, finding the cottage empty, Dunsey steals the money instead.

Silas returns from an errand to find his money gone. Over-whelmed by the loss, he runs to the local tavern for help and announces the theft to a sympathetic audience of tavern regulars. The theft becomes the talk of the village, and a theory arises that the thief might have been a peddler who came through the village some time before. Godfrey, meanwhile, is distracted by thoughts of Dun-sey, who has not returned home. After hearing that Wildfire has been found dead, Godfrey decides to tell his father about the money, though not about his marriage. The Squire flies into a rage at the news, but does not do anything drastic to punish Godfrey.

Silas is utterly disconsolate at the loss of his gold and numbly con-tinues his weaving. Some of the townspeople stop by to offer their condolences and advice. Among these visitors, Dolly Winthrop stands out. Like many of the others, she encourages Silas to go to church—something he has not done since he was banished from Lan-tern Yard—but she is also gentler and more genuinely sympathetic.

Nancy Lammeter arrives at Squire Cass's famed New Year's dance resolved to reject Godfrey's advances because of his unsound character. However, Godfrey is more direct and insistent than he has been in a long time, and Nancy finds herself exhilarated by the evening in spite of her resolution. Meanwhile, Molly, Godfrey's secret wife, is making her way to the Casses' house to reveal the secret marriage. She has their daughter, a toddler, in her arms. Tir-ing after her long walk, Molly takes a draft of opium and passes out by the road. Seeing Silas's cottage and drawn by the light of the fire, Molly's little girl wanders through the open door and falls asleep at Silas's hearth.

Silas is having one of his fits at the time and does not notice the lit-tle girl enter his cottage. When he comes to, he sees her already asleep on his hearth, and is as stunned by her appearance as he was by the disappearance of his money. A while later, Silas traces the girl's foot-steps outside and finds Molly's body lying in the snow. Silas goes to the Squire's house to find the doctor, and causes a stir at the dance when he arrives with the baby girl in his arms. Godfrey, recognizing his daughter, accompanies the doctor to Silas's cottage. When the doctor declares that Molly is dead, Godfrey realizes that his secret is safe. He does not claim his daughter, and Silas adopts her.

Silas grows increasingly attached to the child and names her Eppie, after his mother and sister. With Dolly Winthrop's help, Silas raises the child lovingly. Eppie begins to serve as a bridge between Silas and the rest of the villagers, who offer him help and advice and have come to think of him as an exemplary person because of what he has done. Eppie also brings Silas out of the benumbed state he fell into after the loss of his gold. In his newfound happiness, Silas begins to explore the memories of his past that he has long repressed.

The novel jumps ahead sixteen years. Godfrey has married Nancy and Squire Cass has died. Godfrey has inherited his father's house, but he and Nancy have no children. Their one daughter died at birth, and Nancy has refused to adopt. Eppie has grown into a pretty and spirited young woman, and Silas a contented father. The stone-pit behind Silas's cottage is drained to water neighboring fields, and Dunsey's skeleton is found at the bottom, along with Silas's gold. The discovery frightens Godfrey, who becomes convinced that his own secrets are destined to be uncovered as well. He confesses the truth to Nancy about his marriage to Molly and fathering of Eppie. Nancy is not angry but regretful, saying that they could have adopted Eppie legitimately if Godfrey had told her earlier.

That evening, Godfrey and Nancy decide to visit Silas's cottage to confess the truth of Eppie's lineage and claim her as their daughter. However, after hearing Godfrey and Nancy's story, Eppie tells them she would rather stay with Silas than live with her biological father. Godfrey and Nancy leave, resigning themselves to helping Eppie from afar. The next day Silas decides to visit Lantern Yard to see if he was ever cleared of the theft of which he was accused years before. The town has changed almost beyond recognition, though, and Silas's old chapel has been torn down to make way for a new factory. Silas realizes that his questions will never be answered, but he is content with the sense of faith he has regained through his life with Eppie. That summer Eppie is married to Aaron Winthrop, Dolly's son. Aaron comes to live in Silas's cottage, which has been expanded and refurbished at Godfrey's expense.

CHARACTER LIST

Silas Marner A simple, honest, and kindhearted weaver. After losing faith in both God and his fellow man, Silas lives for fifteen years as a solitary miser. After his money is stolen, his faith and trust are restored by his adopted daughter, Eppie, whom he lovingly raises.

Godfrey Cass The eldest son of Squire Cass. Godfrey is good-natured but selfish and weak-willed. He knows what is right but is unwilling to pay the price for obeying his conscience.

Eppie A girl whom Silas Marner eventually adopts. Eppie is the biological child of Godfrey Cass and Molly Farren, Godfrey's secret wife. Eppie is pretty and spirited, and loves Silas unquestioningly.

Nancy Lammeter The object of Godfrey's affection and his eventual wife. Nancy is pretty, caring, and stubborn, and she lives her life by a code of rules that sometimes seems arbitrary and uncompromising.

Dunstan Cass Godfrey's younger brother. Dunsey, as he is usually called, is cruel, lazy, and unscrupulous, and he loves gambling and drinking.

Squire Cass The wealthiest man in Raveloe. The Squire is lazy, self-satisfied, and short-tempered.

Dolly Winthrop The wheelwright's wife who helps Silas with Eppie. Dolly later becomes Eppie's godmother and mother-in-law. She is kind, patient, and devout.

Molly Farren Godfrey's secret wife and Eppie's mother. Once pretty, Molly has been destroyed by her addictions to opium and alcohol.

William Dane Silas's proud and priggish best friend from his childhood in Lantern Yard. William Dane frames Silas for theft in order to bring disgrace upon him, then marries Silas's fiancée, Sarah.

Mr. Macey Raveloe's parish clerk. Mr. Macey is opinionated and smug but means well.

Aaron Winthrop Dolly's son and Eppie's eventual husband.

Priscilla Lammeter Nancy's homely and plainspoken sister. Priscilla talks endlessly but is extremely competent at everything she does.

Sarah Silas's fiancée in Lantern Yard. Sarah is put off by Silas's strange fit and ends up marrying William Dane after Silas is disgraced.

Mr. Lammeter Nancy's and Priscilla's father. Mr. Lammeter is a proud and morally uncompromising man.

Jem Rodney A somewhat disreputable character and a poacher. Jem sees Silas in the midst of one of Silas's fits. Silas later accuses Jem of stealing his gold.

Mr. Kimble Godfrey's uncle and Raveloe's doctor. Mr. Kimble is usually an animated conversationalist and joker, but becomes irritable when he plays cards. He has no medical degree and inherited the position of village physician from his father.

Mr. Dowlas The town farrier, who shoes horses and tends to general livestock diseases. Mr. Dowlas is a fiercely contrarian person, much taken with his own opinions.

Mr. Snell The landlord of the Rainbow, a local tavern. By nature a conciliatory person, Mr. Snell always tries to settle arguments.

The peddler An anonymous peddler who comes through Raveloe some time before the theft of Silas's gold. The peddler is a suspect in the theft because of his gypsylike appearance—and for lack of a better candidate.

Bryce A friend of both Godfrey and Dunsey. Bryce arranges to buy Wildfire, Dunsey's horse.

Miss Gunns Sisters from a larger nearby town who come to the Squire's New Year's dance. The Misses Gunn are disdainful of Raveloe's rustic ways, but are nonetheless impressed by Nancy Lammeter's beauty.

Sally Oates Silas's neighbor and the wheelwright's wife. Silas eases the pain of Sally's heart disease and dropsy with a concoction he makes out of foxglove.

ANALYSIS OF MAJOR CHARACTERS

SILAS MARNER

The title character, Silas is a solitary weaver who, at the time we meet him, is about thirty-nine years old and has been living in the English countryside village of Raveloe for fifteen years. Silas is reclusive and his neighbors in Raveloe regard him with a mixture of suspicion and curiosity. He spends all day working at his loom and has never made an effort to get to know any of the villagers. Silas's physical appearance is odd: he is bent from his work at the loom, has strange and frightening eyes, and generally looks much older than his years. Because Silas has knowledge of medicinal herbs and is subject to occasional cataleptic fits, many of his neighbors speculate that he has otherworldly powers.

Despite his antisocial behavior, however, Silas is at heart a deeply kind and honest person. At no point in the novel does Silas do or say anything remotely malicious and, strangely for a miser, he is not even particularly selfish. Silas's love of money is merely the product of spiritual desolation, and his hidden capacity for love and sacrifice manifests itself when he takes in and raises Eppie.

Silas's outsider status makes him the focal point for the themes of community, religion, and family that Eliot explores in the novel. As an outcast who eventually becomes Raveloe's most exemplary citizen, Silas serves as a study in the relationship between the individual and the community. His loss and subsequent rediscovery of faith demonstrate both the difficulty and the solace that religious belief can bring. Additionally, the unlikely domestic life that Silas creates with Eppie presents an unconventional but powerful portrait of family and the home.

Though he is the title character of the novel, Silas is by and large passive, acted upon rather than acting on others. Almost all of the major events in the novel demonstrate this passivity. Silas is framed for theft in his old town and, instead of proclaiming his innocence, puts his trust in God to clear his name. Similarly, Dunsey's theft of Silas's gold and Eppie's appearance on Silas's doorstep—rather than any actions Silas takes of his own accord—are the major events that drive the narrative forward. Silas significantly diverges from this pattern of passivity when he decides to keep Eppie, thereby becoming an agent of his eventual salvation.

GODFREY CASS

Godfrey is the eldest son of Squire Cass and the heir to the Cass estate. He is a good-natured young man, but weak-willed and usually unable to think of much beyond his immediate material comfort. As a young man he married an opium addict, Molly Farren, with whom he had a daughter. This secret marriage and Godfrey's handling of it demonstrate the mixture of guilt and moral cowardice that keep him paralyzed for much of the novel. Godfrey consented to the marriage largely out of guilt and keeps the marriage secret because he knows his father will disown him if it ever comes to light.

Despite his physically powerful and graceful presence, Godfrey is generally passive. In this respect he is similar to Silas. However, Godfrey's passivity is different from Silas's, as his endless waffling and indecisiveness stem entirely from selfishness. Godfrey is subject to constant blackmail from Dunsey, who knows of Godfrey's secret marriage, and Godfrey is finally freed of his malicious brother simply by an accident. He is delivered from Molly in a similarly fortuitous way, when Molly freezes to death while en route to Raveloe to expose their marriage to Godfrey's family. Even Godfrey's eventual confession to Nancy is motivated simply by his fright after the discovery of Dunsey's remains. This confession comes years too late—by the time Godfrey is finally ready to take responsibility for Eppie, she has already accepted Silas as her father and does not want to replace him in her life.

NANCY LAMMETER

Nancy is the pretty, caring, and stubborn young lady whom Godfrey pursues and then marries. Like Godfrey, Nancy comes from a family that is wealthy by Raveloe standards. However, her father, unlike Squire Cass, is a man who values moral rectitude, thrift, and hard work. Nancy has inherited these strict values and looks disapprovingly on what she sees as Godfrey's weakness of character. She is, however, exhilarated by Godfrey's attention, in part because of the status he embodies.

Nancy lives her life according to an inflexible code of behavior and belief. She seems to have already decided how she feels about every question that might come up in her life, not necessarily on the basis of any reason or thought, but simply because anything else would represent a sort of weakness in her own eyes. When Nancy is younger, this "code" of hers demands that she and her sister dress alike on formal occasions. When she is older, Nancy's code forbids her to adopt a child, as in her mind such an action represents a defiance of God's plan. Nancy is neither well educated nor particularly curious, and her code marks her as just as much a product of Raveloe's isolation and rusticity as Dolly Winthrop. Nancy is, however, a genuinely kind and caring person, as evidenced by her forgiveness of Godfrey after his confession.

THEMES, MOTIFS & SYMBOLS

THEMES

Themes are the fundamental and often universal ideas explored in a literary work.

THE INDIVIDUAL VERSUS THE COMMUNITY

Silas Marner is in one sense the story of the title character, but it is also very much about the community of Raveloe in which he lives. Much of the novel's dramatic force is generated by the tension between Silas and the society of Raveloe. Silas, who goes from being a member of a tight-knit community to utterly alone and then back again, is a perfect vehicle for Eliot to explore the relationship between the individual and the surrounding community.

In the early nineteenth century, a person's village or town was all-important, providing the sole source of material and emotional support. The notion of interconnectedness and support within a village runs through the novel, in such examples as the parish's charitable allowance for the crippled, the donation of leftovers from the Squire's feasts to the village's poor, and the villagers who drop by Silas's cottage after he is robbed.

The community also provides its members with a structured sense of identity. We see this sense of identity play out in Raveloe's public gatherings. At both the Rainbow and the Squire's dance, interaction is ritualized through a shared understanding of each person's social class and place in the community. As an outsider, living apart from this social structure, Silas initially lacks any sense of this identity. Not able to understand Silas in the context of their community, the villagers see him as strange, regarding him with a mixture of fear and curiosity. Silas is compared to an apparition both when he shows up at the Rainbow and the Red House. To be outside the community is to be something unnatural, even otherworldly.

Though it takes fifteen years, the influence of the community of Raveloe does eventually seep into Silas's life. It does so via Godfrey's problems, which find their way into Silas's cottage first in the form of Dunsey, then again in Eppie. Eliot suggests that the interconnect-edness of community is not something one necessarily enters into voluntarily, nor something one can even avoid. In terms of social standing, Silas and Godfrey are quite far from each other: whereas Silas is a distrusted outsider, Godfrey is the village's golden boy, the heir of its most prominent family. By braiding together the fates of these two characters and showing how the rest of the village becomes implicated as well, Eliot portrays the bonds of community at their most inescapable and pervasive.

CHARACTER AS DESTINY

The plot of *Silas Marner* seems mechanistic at times, as Eliot takes care to give each character his or her just deserts. Dunsey dies, the Squire's lands are divided Godfrey wins Nancy but ends up child-less, and Silas lives happily ever after with Eppie as the most admired man in Raveloe. The tidiness of the novel's resolution may or may not be entirely believable, but it is a central part of Eliot's goal to present the universe as morally ordered. Fate, in the sense of a higher power rewarding and punishing each character's actions, is a central theme of the novel. For Eliot, who we are determines not only what we do, but also what is done to us.

Nearly any character in the novel could serve as an example of this moral order, but perhaps the best illustration is Godfrey. God-frey usually means well, but is unwilling to make sacrifices for what he knows to be right. At one point Godfrey finds himself actually hoping that Molly will die, as his constant hemming and hawing have backed him into so tight a corner that his thoughts have become truly horrible and cruel. However, throughout the novel Eliot maintains that Godfrey is not a bad person—he has simply been compromised by his inaction. Fittingly, Godfrey ends up with a similarly compromised destiny: in his marriage to Nancy he gets what he wants, only to eventually reach the dissatisfied conclusion that it is not what he wanted after all. Godfrey ends up in this ironic situation not simply because he is deserving, but because compro-mised thoughts and actions cannot, in the moral universe of Eliot's novel, have anything but compromised results.

THE INTERDEPENDENCE OF FAITH AND COMMUNITY

In one sense *Silas Marner* can be seen simply as the story of Silas's loss and regaining of his faith. But one could just as easily describe the novel as the story of Silas's rejection and subsequent embrace of his community. In the novel, these notions of faith and community are closely linked. They are both human necessities, and they both feed off of each other. The community of Lantern Yard is united by religious faith, and Raveloe is likewise introduced as a place in which people share the same set of superstitious beliefs. In the typical English village, the church functioned as the predominant social organization. Thus, when Silas loses his faith, he is isolated from any sort of larger community.

The connection between faith and community lies in Eliot's close association of faith in a higher authority with faith in one's fellow man. Silas's regained faith differs from his former Lantern Yard faith in significant ways. His former faith was based first and foremost on the idea of God. When he is unjustly charged with murder, he does nothing to defend himself, trusting in a just God to clear his name. The faith Silas regains through Eppie is different in that it is not even explicitly Christian. Silas does not mention God in the same way he did in Lantern Yard, but bases his faith on the strength of his and Eppie's commitment to each other. In his words, "since . . . I've come to love her . . . I've had light enough to trusten by; and now she says she'll never leave me, I think I shall trusten till I die."

Silas's new faith is a religion that one might imagine Eliot herself espousing after her own break with formalized Christianity. It is a more personal faith than that of Lantern Yard, in which people zealously and superstitiously ascribe supernatural causes to events with straightforward causes, such as Silas's fits. In a sense, Silas's new belief is the opposite of his earlier, simplistic world view in that it preserves the place of mystery and ambiguity. Rather than functioning merely as a supernatural scapegoat, Silas's faith comforts him in the face of the things that do not make sense to him. Additionally, as Dolly points out, Silas's is a faith based on helping others and trusting others to do the same. Both Dolly's and especially Silas's faith consists of a belief in the goodness of other people as much as an idea of the divine. Such a faith is thus inextricably linked to the bonds of community.

MOTIFS

Motifs are recurring structures, contrasts, or literary devices that can help to develop and inform the text's major themes.

THE NATURAL WORLD

Throughout the novel, Eliot draws on the natural world for many images and metaphors. Silas in particular is often compared to plants or animals, and these images are used to trace his progression from isolated loner to well-loved father figure. As he sits alone weaving near the start of the novel, Silas is likened to a spider, solitary and slightly ominous. Just after he is robbed, Silas is compared to an ant that finds its usual path blocked—an image of limitation and confusion, but also of searching for a solution. Later, as Silas begins to reach out to the rest of the village, his soul is likened to a plant, not yet budding but with its sap beginning to circulate. Finally, as he raises Eppie, Silas is described as "unfolding" and "trembling into full consciousness," imagery evoking both the metamorphosis of an insect and the blooming of a flower. This nature imagery also emphasizes the preindustrial setting of the novel, reminding us of a time in England when the natural world was a bigger part of daily life than it was after the Industrial Revolution.

DOMESTICITY

For the most part, the events of *Silas Marner* take place in two homes, Silas's cottage and the Cass household. The novel's two key events are intrusions into Silas's domestic space, first by Dunsey and then by Eppie. Eliot uses the home as a marker of the state of its owner. When Silas is isolated and without faith, his cottage is bleak and closed off from the outside world. As Silas opens himself up to the community, we see that his door is more frequently open and he has a steady stream of visitors. Finally, as Silas and Eppie become a family, the cottage is brightened and filled with new life, both figuratively and in the form of literal improvements and refurbishments to the house and yard. Likewise, the Cass household moves from slovenly and "wifeless" under the Squire to clean and inviting under Nancy.

CLASS

Raveloe, like most of nineteenth-century English society, is organized along strict lines of social class. This social hierarchy is encoded in many ways: the forms characters use to address one another, their habits, even where they sit at social events. While the Casses are not nobility, as landowners they sit atop Raveloe's social pecking order, while Silas, an outsider, is at its base. Nonetheless, Silas proves himself to be the better man than his social superiors. Similarly, in Eppie's view, the simple life of the working class is preferable to that of the landed class. Eliot is skilled in showing how class influences the thinking of her characters, from Dunsey's idea of Silas as simply a source of easy money to Godfrey and Nancy's idea that, as higher-class landowners, their claim to Eppie is stronger than Silas's.

SYMBOLS

Symbols are objects, characters, figures, or colors used to represent abstract ideas or concepts.

SILAS'S LOOM

Silas's loom embodies many of the novel's major themes. On a literal level, the loom is Silas's livelihood and source of income. The extent to which Silas's obsession with money deforms his character is physically embodied by the bent frame and limited eyesight he develops due to so many hours at the loom. The loom also foreshadows the coming of industrialization—the loom is a machine in a time and place when most labor was nonmechanical, related to farming and animal husbandry. Additionally, the loom, constantly in motion but never going anywhere, embodies the unceasing but unchanging nature of Silas's work and life. Finally, the process of weaving functions as a metaphor for the creation of a community, with its many interwoven threads, and presages the way in which Silas will bring together the village of Raveloe.

LANTERN YARD

The place where Silas was raised in a tight-knit religious sect, Lantern Yard is a community of faith, held together by a narrow religious belief that Eliot suggests is based more on superstition than any sort of rational thought. Lantern Yard is the only community Silas knows, and after he is excommunicated, he is unable to find any similar community in Raveloe. Throughout the novel Lantern Yard functions as a symbol of Silas's past, and his gradual coming to grips with what happened there signals his spiritual thaw. When Silas finally goes back to visit Lantern Yard, he finds that the entire neighborhood has disappeared, and no one remembers anything of it. A large factory stands in the spot where the chapel once stood. This disappearance demonstrates the disruptive power of industrialization, which destroys tradition and erases memory. Likewise, this break with the past signals that Silas has finally been able to move beyond his own embittering history, and that his earlier loss of faith has been replaced with newfound purpose.

THE HEARTH

The hearth represents the physical center of the household and symbolizes all of the comforts of home and family. When Godfrey dreams of a life with Nancy, he sees himself "with all his happiness centred on his own hearth, while Nancy would smile on him as he played with the children." Even in a public place such as the Rainbow, one's importance is measured by how close one sits to the fire. Initially, Silas shares his hearth with no one, at least not intentionally. However, the two intruders who forever change Silas's life, first Dunsey and then Eppie, are drawn out of inclement weather by the inviting light of Silas's fire. Silas's cottage can never be entirely separate from the outside world, and the light of Silas's fire attracts both misfortune and redemption. In the end, it is Silas's hearth that feels the warmth of family, while Godfrey's is childless.

SUMMARY & ANALYSIS

PART I, CHAPTERS 1–2

SUMMARY: CHAPTER 1

> *To have sought a medical explanation for this*
> *phenomenon would have been held by Silas himself,*
> *as well as by his minister and fellow-members, a*
> *willful self-exclusion from the spiritual significance*
> *that might lie therein.* (See QUOTATIONS, p. 55)

The novel opens in the English countryside "in the days when the spinning-wheels hummed busily in the farmhouses." In this era one would occasionally encounter weavers—typically pale, thin men who looked like "the remnants of a disinherited race"—beside the hearty peasants who worked in the fields. Because they possessed a special skill and typically had emigrated from larger towns, weavers were invariably outsiders to the peasants among whom they lived. The peasants were superstitious people, often suspicious of both "cleverness" and the world beyond their immediate experience. Thus, the weavers lived isolated lives and often developed the eccentric habits that result from loneliness.

Silas Marner, a linen-weaver of this sort, lives in a stone cottage near a deserted stone-pit in the fictional village of Raveloe. The boys of the village are drawn to the sound of his loom, and often peer through his window with both awe and scorn for his strangeness. Silas responds by glaring at them to scare them away. The boys' parents claim that Silas has special powers, such as the ability to cure rheumatism by invoking the devil. Although Raveloe is a fairly affluent, attractive village, it is far from any major road. Sheltered from currents of progressive thought, the townspeople retain many primitive beliefs.

In the fifteen years Silas has lived in Raveloe, he has not invited any guests into his home, made any effort to befriend other villagers, or attempted to court any of the town's women. Silas's reclusiveness has given rise to a number of myths and rumors among the townspeople. One man swears he once saw Silas in a sort of fit, standing with his limbs stiff and his eyes "set like a dead man's." Mr. Macey, the parish clerk, suggests that such episodes are caused by Silas's soul leaving his body to commune with the devil. Despite these rumors, Silas is never persecuted because the townspeople fear him and because he is indispensable—he is the only weaver in town. As the years pass, local lore also begins to hold that Silas's business has enabled him to save a sizable hoard of money.

Before Silas came to Raveloe, he lived in a town to the north, where he was thought of as a young man "of exemplary life and ardent faith." This town was dominated by a strict religious sect that met in a place called Lantern Yard. During one prayer meeting, Silas became unconscious and rigid for more than an hour, an event that his fellow church members regarded as divinely inspired. However, Silas's best friend at the time, William Dane—a seemingly equally devout but arrogant young man—suggested that Silas's fit might have represented a visitation from the devil rather than from God. Troubled by this suggestion, Silas asked his fiancée, a young servant named Sarah, if she wished to call off their engagement. Though Sarah seemed at first to want to, she did not.

One night Silas stayed up to watch over the senior deacon of Lantern Yard, who was sick. Waiting for William to come in to relieve him at the end of his shift, Silas suddenly realized that it was nearly dawn, the deacon had stopped breathing, and William had never arrived. Silas wondered if he had fallen asleep on his watch. However, later that morning William and the other church members accused Silas of stealing the church's money from the deacon's room. Silas's pocketknife turned up in the bureau where the money had been stored, and the empty money bag was later found in Silas's dwelling. Silas expected God to clear him of the crime, but when the church members drew lots, Silas was determined guilty and excommunicated. Sarah called their engagement off. Crushed, Silas maintained that the last time he used his knife was in William's presence and that he did not remember putting it back in his pocket afterward. To the horror of the church, Silas angrily renounced his religious faith. Soon thereafter, William married Sarah and Silas left town.

SUMMARY: CHAPTER 2

> *Marner's face and figure shrank and bent themselves*
> *into a constant mechanical relation to the objects of*
> *his life, so that he produced the same sort of*
> *impression as a handle or a crooked tube, which has*
> *no meaning standing apart.* (See QUOTATIONS, p. 56)

According to the narrator, Silas finds Raveloe, with its sense of "neglected plenty," completely unlike the world in which he grew up. The fertile soil and climate make farm life much easier in Raveloe than in the barren north, and the villagers are consequently more easygoing and less ardent in their religion. Nothing familiar in Raveloe reawakens Silas's "benumbed" faith in God. Spiritually depleted, Silas uses his loom as a distraction, weaving more quickly than necessary. For the first time he is able to keep the full portion of his earnings for himself, no longer having to share them with an employer or the church. Having no other sense of purpose, Silas feels a sense of fulfillment merely in holding his newly earned money and looking at it.

Around this time Silas notices the cobbler's wife, Sally Oates, suffering the symptoms of heart disease and dropsy, a condition of abnormal swelling in the body. Sally awakens in Silas memories of his mother, who died of similar causes. He offers Sally an herbal preparation of foxglove that his mother had used to ease the pain of the disease. The concoction works, so the villagers conclude that Silas must have some dealings with the occult. Mothers start to bring their sick children to his house to be cured, and men with rheumatism offer Silas silver to cure them. Too honest to play along, Silas sends them all away with growing irritation. The townspeople's hope in Silas's healing power turns to dread, and they come to blame him for accidents and misfortunes that befall them. Having wanted only to help Sally Oates, Silas now finds himself further isolated from his neighbors.

Silas gradually begins to make more money, working sixteen hours a day and obsessively counting his earnings. He enjoys the physical appearance of the gold coins and handles them joyfully. He keeps the coins in an iron pot hidden under the floor beneath his loom, and takes them out only at night, "to enjoy their companionship." When the pot is no longer large enough to hold his hoard, Silas begins keeping the money in two leather bags. He lives this way for fifteen years, until a sudden change alters his life one Christmas.

ANALYSIS: PART I, CHAPTERS 1–2

Eliot opens *Silas Marner* by immediately distancing the novel from its readers. The narrator repeatedly stresses that the time, physical setting, and characters are unfamiliar to us. Eliot evokes the pastoral English countryside of the early nineteenth century, emphasizing Raveloe's distance from large towns and even large roads, an isolation that keeps the town mostly ignorant of the intellectual currents of its own time. The characters behave according to a rustic belief system that is distant and alien to us. This distance is temporal as much as it is spatial. Intervening between the era in which the novel is set and the era in which it is written is the Industrial Revolution. This industrialization dramatically transformed England from a society of farms and villages to one of factories and cities. In *Silas Marner* Eliot is therefore describing a lost world, and part of her purpose in the novel is to evoke what she feels has been lost.

Here, as in all of her novels, Eliot's narrative voice is sympathetic but strongly moral. Eliot does not romanticize the simplicity of her characters. On the contrary, she underlines the flaws and limitations of their worldview with a sort of benevolent condescension. Administering justice by drawing lots, for instance, or suspecting that Silas is allied with Satan because he knows how to work a loom, are clearly outmoded beliefs. However, Eliot also takes it upon herself to explain these characters and their shortcomings—not to justify them, but to make them understandable and human.

Though Silas is isolated, there are hints of his eventual incorporation into the community of Raveloe. Silas's outsider status is partly due to his profession, as, the narrator tells us, weavers of his day were rarely accepted by their neighbors. However, Silas's work also provides a powerful metaphor of unity for that same community. It is Silas who takes the threads spun on Raveloe's individual spinning wheels and weaves them into whole cloth. This work both contrasts with his literal isolation and prefigures a later act, his adoption of Eppie, which serves to unite the community. This metaphor is further reinforced when Chapter Two ends with a comparison of Silas's hermetic existence to a "little shivering thread."

Silas has not always been an outsider. His rejection of community coincides with his loss of faith, and thus, in a sense, his faith in his fellow man has died along with his faith in God. Whereas the religious community in which Silas grew up is founded and governed by a strict belief system, the community of Raveloe shares a looser set of superstitions. When Silas rejects his former beliefs, he begins to idolize his money to fill the void. This spiritually impoverished worship only reinforces his isolation. Money allows Silas to once again worship *something*, but without involving other human beings. When he is banished from his church, he casts away his desire for human fellowship and finds a new source of fulfillment in his gold coins.

Silas's mechanical aptitude and worship of money can be seen as representative of the imminent onset of industrialization, a historical phenomenon that uprooted many people from their villages and tore apart the communities that had previously connected working-class people to one another. The German social philosopher Karl Marx, writing shortly before George Eliot, coined the phrase "the commodification of labor" to describe this uprooting, which tended to dehumanize workers as they came to be defined solely in terms of the monetary value produced by their labor, rather than by their place in a local economy. Silas's existence has become as mechanized as any factory worker's. He is described as shrunken to fit to his loom, so much so that he looks like a part of it, and the narrator compares him to "a handle or a crooked tube, which has no meaning standing apart." Silas's labor holds no significance for him except as a means to collect more of the money he loves. He does not view his work as a contribution to the community or as something in which to take pride. Bereft of connections to other human beings, Silas attributes human qualities to his money, admiring the faces on the coins as if they were friends.

PART I, CHAPTERS 3–4

SUMMARY: CHAPTER 3

Squire Cass is acknowledged as the greatest man in Raveloe, the closest thing the village has to a lord. His sons, however, have "turned out rather ill." The Squire's younger son, Dunstan, more commonly called by the nickname Dunsey, is a sneering and unpleasant young man with a taste for gambling and drinking. The elder son, Godfrey, is handsome and good-natured, and everyone in town wants to see him married to the lovely Nancy Lammeter. Lately, however, Godfrey has been acting strange and looking unwell.

One November afternoon, the two Cass brothers get into a heated argument over 100 pounds that Godfrey has lent Dunsey—money that was the rent from one of their father's tenants. The Squire is growing impatient, Godfrey says, and will soon find out that Godfrey has been lying to him about the rent if Dunsey does not repay the money. Dunsey, however, tells Godfrey to come up with the money himself, lest Dunsey tell their father about Godfrey's secret marriage to the drunken opium addict Molly Farren. Dunsey suggests that Godfrey borrow money or sell his prized horse, Wildfire, at the next day's hunt. Godfrey balks at this, since there is a dance that evening at which he plans to see Nancy. When Dunsey mockingly suggests that Godfrey simply kill Molly off, Godfrey angrily threatens to tell their father about the money and his marriage himself, thus getting Dunsey thrown out of the house along with him.

Godfrey, however, is unwilling to take this step, preferring his uncertain but currently comfortable existence to the certain embarrassment that would result from revealing his secret marriage. Thinking that he has perhaps pushed Godfrey too far, Dunsey offers to sell Godfrey's horse for him. Godfrey agrees to this, and Dunsey leaves. The narrator then gives us a glimpse of Godfrey's future: the empty, monotonous prosperity of the aging country squire who spends his years drinking and wallowing in regret. The narrator adds that Godfrey already has experienced this regret to some degree: we learn that Godfrey was talked into his secret marriage by none other than Dunsey, who used the idea as a trap to gain leverage with which to blackmail Godfrey. Godfrey does genuinely love Nancy Lammeter—as the narrator suggests, Nancy represents everything missing from the household in which Godfrey grew up after his mother's death. The fact that Godfrey cannot act upon his emotions toward Nancy only increases his misery.

SUMMARY: CHAPTER 4

Dunsey sets off the next morning to sell his brother's horse. Passing by Silas Marner's cottage, Dunsey remembers the rumors about Silas's hoard of gold and wonders why he has never thought to persuade Godfrey to ask Silas for a loan. Despite the promise of this idea, Dunsey decides to ride on anyway, since he wants his brother to be upset about having had to sell Wildfire and he looks forward to the bargaining and swagger that will be involved in the sale of the horse.

Dunsey meets some acquaintances who are hunting. After some negotiation he arranges Wildfire's sale, with payment to be handed over upon safe delivery of the horse to the stable. Dunsey decides not to deliver the horse right away, and instead takes part in the hunt, enjoying the prospect of jumping fences to show off the horse. However, Dunsey jumps one fence too many, and Wildfire gets impaled on a stake and dies. No one witnesses the accident, and Dunsey is unhurt, so he makes his way to the road in order to walk home. All the while he thinks of Silas's money. When Dunsey passes Silas's cottage just after dusk and sees a light on through the window, he decides to introduce himself. To his surprise the door is unlocked and the cottage empty. Tempted by the blazing fire inside and the piece of pork roasting over it, Dunsey sits down at the hearth and wonders where Silas is. His thoughts quickly shift to Silas's money and, looking around the cottage, Dunsey notices a spot in the floor carefully covered over with sand. He sweeps away the sand, pries up the loose bricks, and finds the bags of gold. He steals the bags and flees into the darkness.

ANALYSIS: PART I, CHAPTERS 3–4

While the first two chapters establish a tone of monotony and routine, the third chapter introduces narrative tension. Godfrey's secret wife, his frustrated love for Nancy, and Dunsey's blackmail create a precarious situation. Silas's situation is much the opposite: he lives a life marked by unchanging labor and the slow accumulation of money, a life in which change is hard to imagine. The tension between these two lives sets the narrative in motion, as Godfrey's need for money leads Dunsey to Silas's door.

The parallel narratives of Silas and the Cass family do not intersect until Dunsey's theft at the end of Chapter Four. This theft represents the first of three major intersections between Silas and the Cass family. Aside from these three intersections, the two different narratives run along separate tracks, with Eliot following each for a few chapters at a time. This structure of two separate narratives renders each point of intersection significant for both. This first intersection, the theft, sets in motion the action of the entire novel, upsetting the monotony of Silas's life and eventually bringing him forcefully into the life of his surrounding community.

Dunsey's theft bridges not only a narrative distance, but also a social distance. By juxtaposing the wealthy Cass family with the humble Silas, Eliot focuses our attention on the sharp differences in social class within the village of Raveloe. In the nineteenth century, as throughout most of British history, the class system was the predominant reality of village life. The class to which one belonged not only defined one's social interactions, but also shaped one's values and view of the world. Eliot explores class distinctions throughout the novel. All of the characters we meet in the first two chapters are of a lower class than the Cass family, who, while not nobility, still hold a high social rank as landowners. The Casses are admired by everyone in Raveloe and are therefore at the farthest social extreme from Silas, who is seen as the village freak.

For Silas, labor has come to mean nothing more than a way to collect gold coins, while, for the Casses, labor is a completely foreign concept altogether. As a landowner, Squire Cass makes a living not from his own labor but from the rents he collects from his tenants for the right to work his land. This life of ease is especially embodied by Dunsey, who spends his time swapping animals and betting, and who delights in selling his brother's horse. These all represent means of making money without working. When Godfrey needs money, not one of the schemes that occur to Dunsey is rooted in the idea of earning money through toil.

Furthermore, Eliot implies that the Cass family's prosperity, like Godfrey's double life, is not something that can long continue. *Silas Marner* takes place during the Napoleonic Wars, a series of early nineteenth-century conflicts fought by England and various allies against Napoleon's France. These wars kept land prices artificially high. As Eliot writes in Chapter Three, "the fall of prices had not yet come to carry the race of small squires and yeomen down that road to ruin for which extravagant habits and bad husbandry were plentifully anointing their wheels." The metaphor of a carriage poised at the top of a hill, wheels pointed down the slope, is an apt one for the financial and social status of the Cass household. This precarious image of the carriage serves as a counterpoint to the image of Silas's loom, which embodies his steady labor and monotonous life. These images serve to contrast the Cass family's precarious idleness with Silas's persistent, if resigned, industriousness.

PART I, CHAPTERS 5–6

SUMMARY: CHAPTER 5

Silas returns to his cottage, thinking nothing of the unlocked door because he has never been robbed before. He is looking forward to the roast pork, a gift from a customer, which he left cooking while he was running an errand. Noticing nothing out of the ordinary, Silas sits down before his fire. He cannot wait to pull his money out, and decides to lay it on the table as he eats.

Silas removes the bricks and finds the hole under the floorboards empty. He frantically searches the cottage for his gold, desperately hoping that he might have decided to store it someplace else for the night. He eventually realizes that the gold is gone, and he screams in anguish. Silas then tries to think of what could have happened. He initially fears that a greater power removed the money to ruin him a second time, but banishes that thought in favor of the simpler explanation of a robbery. He mentally runs through a list of his neighbors and decides that Jem Rodney, a well-known poacher, might have taken the gold.

Silas decides to declare his loss to the important people of the town, including Squire Cass, in the hopes that they might be able to help recover his money. Silas goes to the Rainbow, the village inn and tavern, to find someone of authority. However, the more prominent citizens of Raveloe are all at the birthday dance we saw Godfrey anticipating earlier, so Silas finds only the "less lofty customers" at the tavern. The Rainbow has two rooms, separating patrons according to their social standing. The parlor, frequented by Squire Cass and others of "select society," is empty. The few hangers-on who are normally permitted into the parlor to enlarge "the opportunity of hectoring and condescension for their betters" are instead taking the better seats in the bar across the hall, to hector and condescend to their inferiors in turn.

SUMMARY: CHAPTER 6

The conversation in the tavern is quite animated by the time Silas arrives, though it has taken a while to get up to speed. The narrator describes this conversation in considerable detail. It begins with an aimless argument about a cow, followed by a story from Mr. Macey about a time when he heard the parson bungle the words of a wedding vow, a story that everyone in the tavern has heard many times before. Macey says that the parson's lapse set him thinking about whether the wedding was therefore invalid and, if not, just what it was that gave weddings meaning in the first place. Just before Silas appears, the conversation lapses back into an argument, this time about the existence of a ghost who allegedly haunts a local stable. The argumentative farrier, Mr. Dowlas, does not believe in the ghost, and offers to stand out in front of the stable all night, betting that he will not see the ghost. He gets no takers, as the Rainbow's landlord, Mr. Snell, argues that some people are just unable to see ghosts.

ANALYSIS: PART I, CHAPTERS 5–6

The theft of Silas's gold forces him to involve himself in the life of the town. This is the second theft we have encountered so far in the novel. The original theft, which drove Silas out of Lantern Yard, made him an outcast from his tight-knit community and deprived him of any faith except in money. The second theft, Dunsey's, eventually reverses both of these effects. Eliot writes that Silas's gold had "gathered his power of loving together into a hard isolation like its own." Its loss makes Silas venture out into the community to ask for help.

The conversation Silas interrupts in the tavern provides Eliot with an opportunity to show a slice of life of the Raveloe community. Almost all of the action thus far in the novel has taken place in the private sphere, within characters' homes. The tavern provides a public counterpart. The Rainbow is the primary meeting place for Raveloe's men, where members of all of the town's social classes meet and mingle. Unlike church, the other significant public space in the town, the tavern is a participatory atmosphere. Everyone is invited to chime in to the arguments and stories. There is, however, a strict hierarchy that is encoded in the interactions we see at the Rainbow. The higher-class patrons order spirits-and-water to drink, the lower-class patrons beer. The higher-class patrons sit near the fire, the lower-class farther away. Even the two rooms of the inn itself are arranged to separate social classes.

The evening's conversation provides examples of the often superstitious beliefs that bind its participants together. In describing the conversation in such painstaking detail, Eliot furnishes not only a vivid rendering of the dialect of the lower class, but also a portrait of their beliefs. The topics of conversation are trivial and the participants are made to seem slightly ridiculous. However, they do occasionally touch on important ideas. Mr. Macey's story concerns the importance of language, and Mr. Snell's point about some people's inability to see ghosts touches on the subjectivity of experience. In simultaneously making light of the denizens of the Rainbow and showing that they possess a certain unschooled curiosity, Eliot tempers her authorial condescension and shows her subjects as limited in certain ways, but nevertheless complex and worthy of attention.

The conversation, however, is a ritual to stave off boredom as much as it is a forum for exchanging beliefs. Like Silas's weaving and the Cass family's hunting and riding, these nightly gatherings at the Rainbow are repetitive. Mr. Macey has told the same story to the same audience many times before. Though this boredom and ritual seem meaningless, they are an integral part of the rural life Eliot presents. These gatherings form the texture of their participants' daily life, a life that is punctuated only occasionally by noteworthy events.

PART I, CHAPTERS 7–8

SUMMARY: CHAPTER 7

Our consciousness rarely registers the beginning of a growth within us any more than without us: there have been many circulations of the sap before we detect the smallest sign of the bud.

(See QUOTATIONS, p. 57)

Silas suddenly appears in the middle of the tavern, his agitation giving him a strange, unearthly appearance. For a moment, everyone present, regardless of his stance in the previous argument about the supernatural, believes he is looking at a ghost. Silas, short of breath after his hurried walk to the inn, finally declares that he has been robbed. The landlord tells Jem Rodney, who is sitting nearest Silas, to seize him, as he is delirious. Hearing the name, Silas turns to Rodney and pleads with him to give his money back, telling him that he will give him a guinea and will not press charges. Rodney reacts angrily, saying that he will not be accused.

The tavern-goers make Silas take off his coat and sit down in a chair by the fire. Everyone calms down, and Silas tells the story of the robbery. The villagers become more sympathetic and believe Silas's story, largely because he appears so crushed and pathetic. The landlord vouches for Jem Rodney, saying that he has been in the inn all evening. Silas apologizes to Rodney, and Mr. Dowlas, the farrier, asks how much money was lost. Silas tells him the exact figure, which is more than 270 pounds. Dowlas suggests that 270 pounds could be carried out easily, and he offers to visit Silas's cottage to search for evidence, since Silas's eyesight is poor and he might have missed something. Dowlas also offers to ask the constable to appoint him deputy-constable, which sets off an argument. Mr. Macey objects that no doctor can also be a constable and that Dowlas—whose duties as a farrier including the treatment of livestock diseases—is a sort of doctor. A compromise is reached wherein Dowlas agrees to act only in an unofficial capacity. Silas then leaves with Dowlas and the landlord to go to the constable's office.

SUMMARY: CHAPTER 8

Godfrey returns home from the dance to find that Dunsey has not yet returned. Godfrey is distracted by thoughts of Nancy Lammeter, and does not think very much about his brother's whereabouts. By morning, everyone is discussing the robbery, and Godfrey and other residents of the village visit Silas's cottage to gather evidence and gossip. A tinder-box is found on the scene and is suspected to be somehow connected to the crime. Though a few villagers suspect that Silas is simply mad or possessed and has lied about the theft, others defend him. Some townspeople suspect that occult forces took the money, and consider clues such as the tinder-box useless.

The tinder-box reminds Mr. Snell, the tavern landlord, of a peddler who had visited Raveloe a month before and had mentioned that he was carrying a tinder-box. The talk among the townspeople turns to determining the peddler's appearance, recalling his "evil looks" and trying to determine whether or not he wore earrings. Everyone is disappointed, however, when Silas says he remembers the peddler's visit but never invited him inside his cottage. Godfrey, remembering the peddler as a "merry grinning fellow," dismisses the stories about the peddler's suspicious character. Silas, however, wanting to identify a specific culprit, clings to the notion of the peddler's guilt.

Dunsey's continuing absence distracts Godfrey from this discussion, and Godfrey worries that Dunsey may have run away with his horse. In an attempt to find out what has happened, Godfrey rides to the town where the hunt started and encounters Bryce, the young man who had agreed to buy Wildfire. Bryce is surprised to learn of Dunsey's disappearance and tells Godfrey that Wildfire has been found dead. Seeing no alternative and hoping to free himself from Dunsey's threats of blackmail, Godfrey decides to tell his father not only about the rent money but about his secret marriage as well. Godfrey steels himself for the worst, as Squire Cass is prone to violent fits of anger and rash decisions that he refuses to rescind, even when his anger has passed. The next morning, Godfrey decides to confess only partly and to try to direct his father's anger toward Dunsey.

ANALYSIS: PART I, CHAPTERS 7–8

Silas's incorporation into Raveloe begins in Chapter 7. His devastation at the loss of his money is evident, and it inspires sympathy in his audience at the tavern. When the news spreads, the village takes an immense interest, based partly on mere curiosity but also on some genuine concern. Whereas he was previously looked upon with a mixture of fear and contempt, Silas is now the object of real sympathy. The townspeople's concern has an effect on Silas, even if at first he does not notice it. As Eliot notes, "Our consciousness rarely registers the beginning of a growth within us any more than without us: there have been many circulations of the sap before we detect the smallest sign of the bud." Silas's incipient bond with the rest of Raveloe is likened to a bud on a plant, a clearly hopeful and positive metaphor of rebirth.

This bond, however, is reinforced only through scapegoating another outsider, the peddler. The townspeople's suspicion of the peddler and their conjectures about his earrings are laughable, but such behavior emphasizes the insularity of the village. The townspeople are deeply suspicious of strangers, especially those with dark skin and earrings who resemble gypsies. However, there is nonetheless some element of logic to these suspicions. As Jem Rodney points out, if a village resident stole the money, it would be quite difficult for him or her to spend it without attracting attention.

Eliot fleshes out Godfrey's character in Chapter Eight, as Godfrey debates whether to come clean to his father. As Eliot writes earlier, Godfrey possesses plenty of "animal courage," but is cursed with "natural irresolution and moral cowardice." He is weak and spoiled, unwilling to make sacrifices for what he knows to be right. Like Dunsey, Godfrey is self-interested and shortsighted: he repeatedly puts off decisions about his future in the hope that his situation will right itself. Unlike the malicious Dunsey, however, Godfrey is basically decent and periodically attempts to do good. Godfrey's resistance to the townspeople's suspicions about the peddler shows that he is at least somewhat free of their antiquated superstitions.

For all his physical grace and strength, Godfrey is a passive character. The one significant act he has taken, marrying Molly Farren, occurred only under pressure from his brother and from Molly herself. Furthermore, even when pushed to act, Godfrey still tends to remain unwilling to own up to the greater consequences of his actions, and is thus left in limbo. Eliot contrasts Godfrey's passivity not only with Dunsey's active malice but also with Squire Cass's violent temper. Like Godfrey, the Squire is lazy and fails to heed his troubles until they are impossible to ignore. The Squire only reaches decisions in fits of anger, making violent and rash resolutions that he refuses to revoke even when his head has cooled. Godfrey, in contrast, never erupts, and merely continues to backpedal.

Though Godfrey is incapable of action, his inaction nonetheless sets events in motion: it frustrates the Squire and Nancy, who wonder why Godfrey has not proposed marriage; it allows Dunsey to take advantage of Godfrey and act in his place; and eventually it forces Molly, and then Silas, into actions of great significance. Ironically, it is thus the perpetually irresolute Godfrey who drives much of the major action of the novel.

PART I, CHAPTERS 9–10

SUMMARY: CHAPTER 9

> [Godfrey] was not likely to be very penetrating in his judgments, but he had always had a sense that his father's indulgence had not been kindness, and had had a vague longing for some discipline that would have checked his own errant weakness and helped his better will. (See QUOTATIONS, p. 58)

Godfrey takes his own breakfast early and waits for Squire Cass to eat and take his morning walk before speaking with him. Godfrey tells his father about Wildfire and about how he gave the rent money to Dunsey. His father flies into one of his rages and asks why Godfrey stole from him and lied to him for Dunsey's sake. When Godfrey is evasive, the Squire comes close to guessing the truth. The Squire goes on and on, blaming his current financial troubles on the overindulgence of his sons. Godfrey insists that he has always been willing to help with the management of his father's estate, but the Squire changes the subject, complaining about Godfrey's waffling over whether to marry Nancy Lammeter. The Squire offers to propose for Godfrey, but Godfrey is again evasive and refuses the offer. Afterward, Godfrey is not sure whether to be grateful that nothing seems to have changed or uneasy that he has had to tell more half-truths. Though Godfrey worries that his father might push his hand and force him to refuse Nancy, as usual, he merely places his trust in "Favourable Chance," hoping that some unforeseen event will rescue him from his predicament.

SUMMARY: CHAPTER 10

Weeks pass with no new evidence about the robbery and no sign of Dunsey. No one connects Dunsey's disappearance with the theft, however, and the peddler remains the primary suspect, though some still insist that an inexplicable otherworldly force is responsible. Silas is still inconsolable, and passes the days weaving joylessly. Without his money, his life feels empty and purposeless. He earns the pity of the villagers, who now think of him as helpless rather than dangerous. They bring Silas food, call on him to offer condolences, and try to help him get over his loss. These efforts are only mildly successful. Mr. Macey subjects Silas to a long and discursive speech about coming to church, among other things, but gets little reaction and leaves more perplexed by Silas than before.

Another visitor is Dolly Winthrop, the wheelwright's wife, a selfless and patient woman. Dolly brings her son Aaron and some of her famed lard-cakes. She encourages Silas to attend church, particularly since it is Christmastime. When she asks if he has ever been to church, Silas responds that he has not; he has only been to chapel. Dolly does not understand the distinction Silas is making—nor, in any significant way, does Silas. Wanting to show his gratitude for the visit, all Silas can think to do is offer Aaron a bit of lard-cake. Aaron is frightened of Silas, but Dolly coaxes him into singing a Christmas carol. Despite his gratitude, Silas is relieved after the two have left and he is alone to weave and mourn the loss of his money.

Silas does not go to church on Christmas Day, but almost everyone else in town does. The Casses hold a family Christmas party that night, and invite the Kimbles, Godfrey's aunt and uncle. All evening Godfrey looks forward longingly to the Squire's famed New Year's dance and the chance to be with Nancy. The prospect of Dunsey's return looms over Godfrey, but he tries to ignore it.

ANALYSIS: PART I, CHAPTERS 9–10

Though Eliot has already described Squire Cass's parties, house, and temper tantrums, Godfrey's confrontation with his father is the first time we actually encounter the "greatest man in Raveloe." He is not, we soon discover, "great" in any real sense. The Squire is complacent, lazy, arrogant, and not particularly bright, having spent his life—merely by good fortune of birth—as the biggest fish in a very small pond. He does not have as much money as he once did and has spoiled his sons—not, it seems, out of affection, but simply out of neglect. The Squire is the only role model Godfrey has had while growing up, and Godfrey's shortcomings can be seen as stemming at least in part from his father's.

Chapter 10 returns us to Silas's domestic existence, and we see that he is overwhelmed by the void the robbery has left in his life. Though his life before the theft might have appeared empty and sad, it was nonetheless "an eager life, filled with immediate purpose that fenced him in from the wide, cheerless unknown." Likewise, though Silas's money was, according to the narrator, a "dead disrupted thing," it nonetheless had given him purpose in life and satisfied his need for connection and meaning. Now, however, Silas is broken and utterly defenseless in the face of an outside world that he long ago rejected as corrupt and uncaring. Once again, his most valued possession has been taken from him.

Like her earlier comparison of Silas to a budding plant, Eliot's imagery in this chapter gives us hope for Silas's recovery. The progression of imagery Eliot uses is largely drawn from nature. Silas initially clings to his money as to the roots of a plant, and now is confused like "a plodding ant when the earth has broken away on its homeward path." Finally, Eliot foreshadows a metaphor she uses later: Silas is "still the shrunken rivulet, with only this difference, that its little groove of sand was blocked up, and it wandered confusedly against dark obstruction." The three phenomena to which Silas is compared in these metaphors share a common aspect of recovery and self-righting. The roots of the plant will regrow in new soil, the ant will find its way, and the dammed stream will rise with water until it flows over its obstruction.

Dolly Winthrop provides a simple, compelling portrait of religious faith. Like the philosophical fumblings of the Rainbow's denizens, the "simple Raveloe theology" that Dolly professes to Silas is something at which a seminarian might scoff. Dolly is illiterate and thus does not even understand the words of some of the Christmas carols she so loves. Nonetheless, Dolly's description of her faith is eloquent in its own way. By placing her faith in "Them as are above us" while at the same time demanding that "we'n done our part," Dolly holds to a distinctly community-oriented faith. For Dolly, faith in God provides not only an incentive to do good works herself, but also a trust that others in the community will do their part.

Dolly's beliefs contrast markedly with the "Favourable Chance" relied upon by Godfrey and other men "who follow their own devices instead of obeying a law they believe in." In Dolly's Christianity, the requirement of action goes a long way toward fulfilling the expectations of faith. Godfrey's faith, while perhaps more sophisticated than Dolly's, seems far more futile.

PART I, CHAPTERS 11–12

SUMMARY & ANALYSIS

SUMMARY: CHAPTER 11

Nancy Lammeter and her father arrive at the Red House for the Squire's New Year's dance. The trip over slushy roads has not been an easy one, and Nancy is annoyed that she has to let Godfrey help her out of her carriage. Nancy thinks she has made it clear that she does not wish to marry Godfrey. His unwelcome attention bothers her, though the way he often ignores her bothers her just as much. Nancy makes her way upstairs to a dressing room that she must share with six other women, including the Gunn sisters, who come from a larger town and regard Raveloe society with disdain. Mrs. Osgood, an aunt of whom Nancy is fond, is also among the women. As she puts on her dress for the dance, Nancy impresses the Gunn sisters as a "rustic beauty"—lovely and immaculate but, with her rough hands and slang, clearly ignorant of the higher social graces.

Nancy's sister Priscilla arrives and complains about how Nancy always insists they wear matching gowns. Priscilla freely admits she is ugly and, in doing so, manages to imply that the Gunns are ugly as well. However, Priscilla insists that she has no desire to marry anyway. When Nancy says that she doesn't want to marry either, Priscilla pooh-poohs her. When they go down to the parlor, Nancy accepts a seat between Godfrey and the rector, Mr. Crackenthorp. She cannot help but feel exhilarated by the prospect that she could be the mistress of the Red House herself. Nancy reminds herself, however, that she does not care for Godfrey's money or status because she finds him of unsound character. She blushes at these thoughts. The rector notices and points out her blush to Godfrey. Though Godfrey determinedly avoids looking at Nancy, the half-drunk Squire tries to help things along by complimenting Nancy's beauty. After a little more banter, the Squire pointedly asks Godfrey if he has asked Nancy for the first dance of the evening. Godfrey replies that he has not, but nonetheless embarrassedly asks Nancy, and she accepts.

The fiddler comes in, and, after playing a few preludes, he leads the guests into the White Parlour, where the dancing begins. Mr. Macey and a few other townspeople sit off to one side, commenting on the dancers. They notice Godfrey escorting Nancy off to the adjoining smaller parlor, and assume that the two are going "sweethearting." In reality, Nancy has torn her dress and has asked to sit down to wait for her sister to help mend it. Nancy tells Godfrey that she doesn't want to go into the smaller room with him and will just wait on her own. He insists that she will be more comfortable there and offers to leave. To her own exasperation, Nancy is as annoyed as she is relieved by Godfrey's offer. He tells Nancy that dancing with her means very much to him and asks if she would ever forgive him if he changed his ways. She replies that it would be better if no change were necessary. Godfrey, aware that Nancy still cares for him, tells Nancy she is hard-hearted, hoping to provoke a quarrel. Just then, however, Priscilla arrives to fix the hem of Nancy's dress. Godfrey, exhilarated by the opportunity to be near Nancy, decides to stay with them rather than go back to the dance.

SUMMARY: CHAPTER 12

While Godfrey is at the dance, his wife Molly is approaching Raveloe on foot with their baby daughter in her arms. Godfrey has told Molly that he would rather die than acknowledge her as his wife. She knows there is a dance being held at the Red House and plans to crash the party in order to get revenge against Godfrey. Molly is addicted to opium and knows that this, not Godfrey, is the primary reason for her troubles, but she also resents Godfrey's wealth and comfort and believes that he should support her.

Molly has been walking since morning, and, as evening falls, she begins to tire in the snow and cold. To comfort herself, she takes a draft of opium. The drug makes her drowsy, and after a while she passes out by the side of the road, still holding the child. As Molly's arms relax, the little girl wakes up and sees a light moving. Thinking it is a living thing, she tries to catch the light but fails. She follows it to its source, which is the fire in Silas Marner's nearby cottage. The child toddles through the open door, sits down on the hearth, and soon falls asleep, content in the warmth of the fire.

In the weeks since the theft, Silas has developed a habit of opening his door and looking out distractedly, as if he might somehow see his gold return, or at least get some news of it. On New Year's Eve he is particularly agitated and opens the door repeatedly. The last time he does so, he stands and looks out for a long time, but does not see what is actually coming toward him at that instant: Molly's child. As he turns to shut the door again, Silas has one of his cataleptic fits, and stands unaware and unmoving with his hand on the open door. When he comes out of the fit—as always, unaware that it has even occurred—he shuts the door.

As Silas walks back inside, his eyes nearsighted and weak from his years of close work at the loom, he sees what he thinks is his gold on the floor. He leans forward to touch the gold, but finds that the object under his fingers is soft—the blonde hair of the sleeping child. Silas kneels down to examine the child, thinking for a moment that his little sister, who died in childhood, has been brought back to him. This memory of his sister triggers a flood of other memories of Lantern Yard, the first he has had in many years. These memories occupy Silas until the child wakes up, calling for her mother. Silas reheats some of his porridge, sweetening it with the brown sugar he has always denied himself, and feeds it to the child, which quiets her. Finally, seeing the child's wet boots, it occurs to Silas to wonder where she came from, and he follows her tracks along the road until he finds her mother's body lying in the snow.

ANALYSIS: PART I, CHAPTERS 11–12

The appearance of the little girl on Silas's hearth is the second of the three intersections between the parallel narratives of Silas and the Cass family. Like the first intersection, the theft of Silas's gold, it is one of the novel's two major turning points. Her appearance will at once fill Silas's sense of loss and resume his process of reentering the community. The fact that Silas first mistakes the little girl for his gold—previously the central driving force of his life—foreshadows the strength of the bond that Silas will soon forge with the girl.

Several details of the girl's arrival link the event to the two earlier turning points in Silas's life—his expulsion from his religious sect and the theft of his gold. Like Dunsey, the little girl passes by Silas's cottage in inclement weather, feels drawn to the cottage by the light of the fire, and enters without Silas's knowledge. In addition, just as Silas's fit rendered him unaware that William Dane had framed him for theft in Lantern Yard, another fit renders him unaware of the little girl's arrival. Significantly, in all three of these key events, Silas is passive, not active—he is framed, he is robbed, he is standing with the door open when a child toddles in from a snowstorm.

A key symbolic difference between Dunsey's visit and the little girl's, however, is that Silas opens the door himself this time. Even though he opens the door only to peer out into the darkness after his lost gold, and though he is unaware that the girl actually enters, Silas's act of standing at his open door contrasts markedly with his previous habits. Silas was once a man obsessed with isolation—

closing his shutters, locking his doors, and viewing his customers as nothing more than a means to acquire more money. In opening his door, Silas symbolically opens himself up to the outside world from which he has lived apart for so long. As Silas realizes, if only vaguely, in Chapter 10, "if any help came to him it must come from without."

It is not until this point, halfway through the novel, that we meet the last two of the major characters: Nancy Lammeter and the little girl who will become known as Eppie. Eppie does not develop as a true character until she grows up a bit. However, we learn much about Nancy's character in the first scene in which she appears, the Squire's New Year's dance. We have already heard much about Nancy, especially her beauty. Thus, not surprisingly, Nancy's introduction focuses on her appearance, specifically on how her beauty is still evident despite her muddy raincoat and the frightened expression on her face. This opening image is fitting for Nancy, who is called a "rustic beauty." Though blessed with natural grace and poise, Nancy is unpolished—her speech is somewhat vulgar, her hands are calloused, and she has had little formal schooling. Thus, though Nancy is separated from Silas and his neighbors by degrees of wealth and privilege, she is no less a product of Raveloe's sleepy isolation. Like the poorer townspeople, she has created her own code of conduct and beliefs from a mix of religion and superstition. However, like her upstanding, almost priggish father, Nancy displays a Calvinist severity in her judgments, frowning on Godfrey's weakness of character and attempting to curb her feelings for him. Nancy stubbornly holds to these beliefs, with one exception—we see her conspicuously waver in her attitude toward Godfrey.

PART I, CHAPTERS 13–15

SUMMARY: CHAPTER 13

Back at the Red House, the men dance and Godfrey stands to the side of the parlor to admire Nancy. Godfrey suddenly notices Silas Marner enter carrying Godfrey's child, and, shocked, he walks over with Mr. Lammeter and Mr. Crackenthorp to discover what has brought Silas here. The Squire angrily questions Silas, asking him why he has intruded. Silas says he is looking for the doctor because he has found a woman, apparently dead, lying near his door. Knowing that it is Molly, Godfrey is terrified that perhaps she is not in fact dead. Silas's appearance causes a stir, and the guests are told simply that a woman has been found ill. When Mrs. Kimble suggests that Silas leave the girl at the Red House, Silas refuses, claiming that she came to him and is his to keep.

Godfrey insists on accompanying the doctor, Mr. Kimble, to Silas's cottage, and they pick up Dolly along the way to serve as a nurse. Kimble's title is "Mr." rather than "Dr." because he has no medical degree and inherited his position as village doctor. Godfrey waits outside the cottage in agony, realizing that if Molly is dead he is free to marry Nancy, but that if Molly lives he has to confess everything. When Kimble comes out, he declares that the woman has been dead for hours. Godfrey insists on seeing her, claiming to Kimble that he had seen a woman of a similar description the day before. As he verifies that the woman is in fact Molly, Godfrey sees Silas holding the child and asks him if he intends to take the child to the parish. Silas replies that he wants to keep her, since both he and she are alone, and without his gold he has nothing else to live for. He implies a connection between his lost money, "gone, I don't know where," and the baby, "come from I don't know where." Godfrey gives Silas money to buy clothes for the little girl, and then hurries to catch up with Mr. Kimble.

Godfrey tells Kimble that the dead woman is not the woman he saw before. The two talk about the oddness of Silas wanting to keep the child, and Kimble says that if he were younger he might want the child for himself. Godfrey's thoughts turn to Nancy, and how he can now court her without dread of the consequences. He sees no reason to confess his previous marriage to her, and vows that he will see to it that his daughter is well cared for. Godfrey tells himself that the girl might be just as happy without knowing him as her father.

SUMMARY: CHAPTER 14

Molly is given an anonymous pauper's burial, but her death, the narrator notes, will have great consequences for the inhabitants of Raveloe. The villagers are surprised by Silas's desire to keep the child, and once again they become more sympathetic toward him. Dolly is particularly helpful, offering advice, giving him clothing outgrown by her own children, and helping to bathe and care for the girl. Silas is grateful but makes clear that he wishes to learn to do everything himself, so that the little girl will be attached to him from the start. Silas remains amazed by the girl's arrival and continues to think that in some way his gold has turned into the child.

Dolly persuades Silas to have the child baptized, though at first Silas does not really know what the ceremony means. Dolly tells him to come up with a name for her and he suggests Hephzibah, the name of his mother and sister. Dolly is skeptical, saying that it doesn't sound like a "christened name" and is a little long. Silas surprises her by responding that it is in fact a name from the Bible. He adds that his little sister was called Eppie for short.

Eppie and Silas are baptized together, and Silas finds that the child brings him closer to the other villagers. Unlike his gold, which exacerbated his isolation and did not respond to his attentions, young Eppie is endlessly curious and demanding. Her desires are infectious, and as she hungrily explores the world around her, so does Silas. Whereas his gold had driven him to stay indoors and work endlessly, Eppie tempts Silas away from his work to play outside. In the spring and summer, when it is sunny, Silas takes Eppie to the fields of flowers beyond the stone-pit and sits and watches her play. Silas's growth mirrors Eppie's, and he begins to explore memories and thoughts he has kept locked away for many years.

By the time Eppie is three, she shows signs of mischievousness, and Dolly insists that Silas not spoil her: he should punish her either by spanking her or by putting her in the coal-hole to frighten her. Shortly after this conversation, Eppie escapes from the cottage and goes missing for a while, though she is soon found. Despite his relief at finding her, Silas decides that he must be stern with Eppie. His use of the coal-hole is ineffective, however, as Eppie takes a liking to the place.

Thus, Eppie is reared without punishment. Silas is even reluctant to leave her with anyone else and so takes her with him on his rounds to gather yarn. Eppie becomes an object of fascination and affection, and, as a result, so does Silas. Instead of looking at him with repulsion, the townspeople now offer advice and encouragement. Even children who had formerly found Silas frightening take a liking to him. Silas, in turn, takes an active interest in the town, wanting to give Eppie all that is good in the village. Moreover, Silas no longer hoards his money. Since his gold was stolen, he has lost the sense of pleasure he once felt at counting and touching his savings. Now, with Eppie, he realizes he has found something greater.

SUMMARY: CHAPTER 15
Godfrey keeps a distant eye on Eppie. He gives her the occasional present but is careful not to betray too strong an interest. He does

not feel particularly guilty about failing to claim her because he is confident that she is being taken care of well. Dunsey still has not returned, and Godfrey, released from his marriage and doubtful that he will ever hear from his brother again, can devote himself to freely wooing Nancy. He begins to spend more time at Nancy's home, and people say that he has changed for the better. Godfrey promises himself that his daughter will always be well cared for, even though she is in the hands of the poor weaver.

ANALYSIS: PART I, CHAPTERS 13–15

The parallels between the novel's two pivotal events are further developed in this section. Like the theft, Eppie's arrival again drives Silas to interrupt a public gathering in a dramatic fashion, this time at the Red House rather than the Rainbow. Both appearances cause quite a commotion, and both times Silas arrives with an otherworldly aura. At the Rainbow, the assembled men all take Silas for a ghost. Similarly, when Silas appears with Eppie at the dance, Godfrey is as shocked as if he is seeing an "apparition from the dead." Both scenes emphasize Silas's outsider status. Both the tavern and the Squire's dance are governed by rules of hierarchy and habit in which everyone relies on "safe, well-tested personalities." In these comfortable, ritualized spaces, Silas's entrances are as disruptive and disorienting as visits from a ghost.

Silas, too, is understandably disoriented by the appearance of Eppie. He continues to associate her with his gold and believes, in a vague way, that his gold has somehow turned into her. In a way, of course, Silas's connection is correct, as both the gold's disappearance and Eppie's appearance can be indirectly traced to Godfrey and his secret marriage. More important, the fact that Silas equates Eppie with the gold indicates that she has effectively replaced his gold as the object of his affections.

However, whereas the gold isolated Silas, Eppie becomes a bridge between him and the rest of the world. Not only does she return his affection in a way that his guineas never could, but her desire and curiosity about the world ignite similar feelings in Silas. Eliot uses the weather as a signal of this change. Whereas Dunsey stole the gold on a rainy night and Eppie appeared in a blizzard, the afternoons that Silas and Eppie spend together at play are sunny and warm. Also, Eliot once again uses a metaphor from the natural world to describe Silas's growth. As he begins to come out of his isolation and self-denial, Silas's soul is likened to a metamorphosing butterfly or budding flower, unfolding and "trembling gradually into full consciousness."

Godfrey is at his worst in these chapters. While it is clear that he is not directly responsible for Molly's death, Godfrey's desperate desire that Molly not survive is horrifyingly cruel and selfish. Eliot, always uncompromising in her moral judgments, presents Godfrey's cruelty as the natural result of his dishonesty and cowardice. This selfishness is simply the result of Godfrey being "a man whose happiness hangs on duplicity," who repeatedly shirks the demands of his conscience. Strangely enough, however, Godfrey seems to be rewarded for his duplicity, as he receives exactly the miracle for which he has hoped. It is not difficult for us to surmise, though, that Godfrey will not get off quite so easily.

As mentioned earlier, both of the novel's main characters, Silas and Godfrey, are remarkable for their passivity. Neither man acts— instead, both are by and large acted upon. However, Silas is acted upon primarily because of bad luck, whereas Godfrey is acted upon because of his own naïveté and cowardice. Here, both characters are presented with an opportunity for action. Silas takes action, while Godfrey does not. Silas's decision to keep Eppie has great positive consequences for him, bringing him companionship and redemption. Godfrey could have made the same decision—as Eppie's natural father, with greater justification—but he does not. As we will see, when Godfrey eventually tries to make up for this inaction, it will be too late.

PART II, CHAPTERS 16–18

SUMMARY: CHAPTER 16

The action resumes sixteen years later, as the Raveloe congregation files out of church after a Sunday service. Godfrey has married Nancy, and though they have aged well, they no longer look young. Squire Cass has died, but his inheritance was divided after his death, and Godfrey did not inherit the title of Squire. Silas Marner is also in the departing congregation. His eyes have a more focused look than they did before, but otherwise he looks quite old for a man of fifty-five. Eppie, eighteen and quite pretty, walks beside Silas, while Aaron Winthrop follows them eagerly. Eppie tells Silas that she wants a garden, and Aaron offers to dig it for them. They decide that

Aaron should come to their cottage to mark it out that afternoon, and that he should bring his mother, Dolly.

Silas and Eppie return to the cottage, which has changed greatly since we last saw it. There are now pets: a dog, a cat, and a kitten. The cottage now has another room and is decorated with oak furniture, courtesy of Godfrey. We learn that the townspeople always note Godfrey's kindness toward Silas and Eppie with approval and that they now regard Silas as an "exceptional person." Mr. Macey even claims that Silas's good deed of adopting Eppie will bring back the stolen gold someday. Having returned home, Silas and Eppie eat dinner. Silas watches Eppie play with the pets as she eats.

After dinner, Silas and Eppie go outside so that Silas can smoke his pipe. The pipe is a habit that Silas's neighbors have suggested as a possible remedy for his cataleptic fits. Though Silas finds tobacco disagreeable, he continues with the practice, going along with his neighbors' advice. Silas's adoption of Raveloe customs such as smoking, the narrator tells us, is matched by a growing acknowledgement of his own past. Silas has gradually been telling Dolly Winthrop the story of his previous life in Lantern Yard. Dolly is intrigued and puzzled by the customs he describes. They both try to make sense of the practice of drawing lots to mete out justice, and attempt to understand how Silas could have been falsely convicted by this method.

We learn that Silas has also discussed his past with Eppie. He has informed her that he is not her father and has told her how she came to him at her mother's death. She is not unduly troubled by the story and does not wonder about her father, as she considers Silas a better father than any other in Raveloe. She is, however, eager to know things about her mother, and repeatedly asks Silas to describe what little he knows of her. Silas has given Eppie her mother's wedding ring, which she often gets out to look at.

As the two come out of the cottage for Silas's smoke, Silas mentions that the garden will need a wall to keep the animals out. Eppie suggests building a wall out of stones, so she goes to the stone-pit, where she notices that the water level has dropped. Silas tells her that the pit is being drained in order to water neighboring fields. Eppie tries to carry a stone, but it is heavy and she lets it drop. Sitting down with Silas, Eppie tells him that Aaron Winthrop has spoken of marrying her. Silas conceals his sadness at this news. Eppie adds that Aaron has offered Silas a place to live in their household if they are married. Eppie says she is reluctant, as she does not want her life to change at all, but Silas tells her that she will eventually need someone younger than he to take care of her. Silas suggests that they speak to Dolly, who is Eppie's godmother, about the matter.

SUMMARY: CHAPTER 17

Meanwhile, the Red House has likewise gained a much more domestic feel than it had during the Squire's "wifeless reign." Nancy invites Priscilla and their father to stay at the Red House for tea, but Priscilla declines, saying she has work to do at home. Priscilla has taken over management of the Lammeter farm from her aging father. Before Priscilla leaves, she and Nancy take a walk around the garden. Nancy mentions that Godfrey is not contented with their domestic life. This angers Priscilla, but Nancy rushes to defend Godfrey, saying it is only natural that he should be disappointed at not having any children.

Godfrey goes on his customary Sunday afternoon walk around his grounds and leaves Nancy with her thoughts. Nancy muses, as she often does, on their lack of children and the disappointment it has caused Godfrey. They did have one daughter, but she died at birth. Nancy wonders whether she was right to resist Godfrey's suggestion that they adopt. She has been adamant in her resistance, insisting that it is not right to seek something that Providence had withheld and predicting that an adopted child would inevitably turn out poorly. Like her insistence years before that she and Priscilla wear the same dress, Nancy's unyielding opposition to adoption is not based on any particular reasoning, but simply because she feels it important to have "her unalterable little code." Godfrey's argument—that the adopted Eppie has turned out well—is of no use. Never considering that Silas might object, Godfrey has all along specified that if he and Nancy were to adopt, they should adopt Eppie. Considering his childless home a retribution for failing to claim Eppie, Godfrey sees adopting her as a way to make up for his earlier fault.

SUMMARY: CHAPTER 18

I can't say what I should have done about that,
Godfrey. I should never have married anybody else.
But I wasn't worth doing wrong for—nothing is in
this world. Nothing is so good as it seems
beforehand—not even our marrying wasn't, you see.
(See QUOTATIONS, p. 59)

Godfrey returns from his walk, trembling, and tells Nancy to sit down. He tells her that the skeleton of his brother Dunsey has been found in the newly drained stone-pit behind Silas's cottage. The body has been there for sixteen years, and it is clear that it was Dunsey who robbed Silas. Dunsey fell into the pit as he made his escape, and the money has been found with his remains. Godfrey is greatly shaken by the discovery, and it convinces him that all hidden things eventually come to light. Thus, Godfrey goes on to make his own confession, telling Nancy of his secret marriage to Molly and of Eppie's true lineage. Nancy responds not angrily but instead with regret, saying that had she known the truth about Eppie, she would have consented to adopt her six years before. Nancy and Godfrey resolve to do their duty now and make plans to visit Silas Marner's cottage that evening.

ANALYSIS: PART II, CHAPTERS 16–18

Silas's transition into the community is complete by this point in the novel. Now he is not only a full member of the Raveloe community, but is universally considered its most exemplary citizen. Even the most fractious town gossips look upon Silas with respect. Importantly, much as the town has gotten to know Silas better, so have we. In his interactions with Eppie in this section, Silas speaks more than he has anywhere else in the book and even displays a bit of a sense of humor. Additionally, as he opens up to pipe smoking and other town customs and beliefs, he also begins to explore his past. Silas attempts to attain new self-knowledge and to reconcile his old religious beliefs with his new ones.

The device of the fifteen-year time lapse serves to balance the novel and matches the earlier fifteen-year lapse between Silas's arrival in Raveloe and the events that form the heart of the novel. The events that follow this second jump in time are thus much like an epilogue. The characters are all older, and times are changing: the profession of the weaver is even becoming obsolete. While these final chapters do contain action and plot development, they represent the logical continuation of events already set in motion and thus, to a certain extent, already determined. Even Godfrey's confession, which seems a striking departure from his lifetime of prevarication, is drawn out of him by the shock of the discovery of Dunsey's death, an event that occurred years before. Importantly, because the narrative time lapse implies that we have passed a point of no return, we are left suspicious of Godfrey's chances of getting Eppie back.

Here, Eppie also emerges for the first time as a real character, and Eliot uses her character to return to the topic of social class. The child of nobility raised in poverty is a staple narrative device in literature, from Elizabethan comedy to Victorian melodrama. Here, Eliot uses Eppie to play with the conventions of this narrative device. With her "touch of refinement and fervour," Eppie is not quite a "common village maiden." However, instead of attributing Eppie's refinement to her genteel lineage, Eliot ascribes it to the "tender and peculiar love" with which Silas has raised her. The implication is that Eppie's upbringing has been far more important than her heredity, and that she is a better person than she would have been if Silas had not raised her.

The discovery of Dunsey's remains underlines the small, closed nature of Eliot's narrative universe. Far from having left the country or joined the army, as the townspeople have speculated, it turns out that Dunsey has been in Raveloe all along. In fact, ironically, Silas is the only major character we have seen enter or leave Raveloe in the entire novel. Eliot emphasizes this hermetic quality of existence in Raveloe partly to portray the inertia of English rural life. However, Eliot also wishes this insularity to evoke a world where one can never escape the repercussions of the past or the effects of one's actions. In Raveloe, things do not simply go away.

PART II, CHAPTERS 19–21, CONCLUSION

SUMMARY: CHAPTER 19

Eppie and Silas sit in their cottage later that evening. Silas has sent Dolly and Aaron Winthrop away, desiring solitude with his daughter after the excitement of the afternoon's discovery. Silas muses about the return of his money and reconsiders the events that have passed since he lost it. He tells Eppie how he initially hoped she might somehow turn back into the gold, but later grew fearful of that that prospect because he loved her more than the money. Silas tells Eppie how much he loves her, and says the money has simply been "kept till it was wanted for you." She responds that if not for Silas, she would have been sent to the workhouse.

Someone knocks at the door, and Eppie opens it to find Godfrey and Nancy Cass. Godfrey tells Silas that he wants to make up to Silas not only for what Dunsey did, but also for another debt he owes to the weaver. Godfrey tells Silas that the money is not enough for him to live on without continuing to work. Silas, however, argues that though it might seem like a very small sum to a gentleman, it is more money than many other working people have. Godfrey says that Eppie does not look like she was born for a working life and that she would do better living in a place like his home. Silas becomes uneasy.

Godfrey explains that since they have no children, they would like Eppie to come live with them as their daughter. He assumes that Silas would like to see Eppie in such an advantageous position, and promises that Silas will be provided for himself. Eppie sees that Silas is distressed, though Silas tells her to do as she chooses. Eppie tells Godfrey and Nancy that she does not want to leave her father, nor does she want to become a lady.

Godfrey insists that he has a claim on Eppie and confesses that he is her father. Silas angrily retorts that, if this is the case, Godfrey should have claimed Eppie when she was a baby instead of waiting until Silas and Eppie had grown to love each other. Not expecting this resistance, Godfrey tells Silas that he is standing in the way of Eppie's welfare. Silas says that he will not argue anymore and leaves the decision up to Eppie. As she listens, Nancy cannot help but sympathize with Silas and Eppie, but feels that it is only right that Eppie claim her birthright. Nancy feels that Eppie's new life would be an unquestionably better one. Eppie, however, says that she would rather stay with Silas. Nancy tells her that it is her duty to go to her real father's house, but Eppie responds that Silas is her real father. Godfrey, greatly discouraged, turns to leave, and Nancy says they will return another day.

SUMMARY: CHAPTER 20

Godfrey and Nancy return home and realize that Eppie's decision is final. Godfrey concedes that what Silas has said is right, and he resigns himself simply to helping Eppie from afar. Godfrey and Nancy surmise that Eppie will marry Aaron, and Godfrey wistfully comments on how pretty and nice Eppie seemed. He says he noticed that Eppie took a dislike to him when he confessed that he was her father, and he decides that it must be his punishment in life to be disliked by his daughter. Godfrey tells Nancy that he is grateful, despite everything, to have been able to marry her, and vows to be satisfied with their marriage.

SUMMARY: CHAPTER 21

The next morning Silas tells Eppie that he wants to make a trip to his old home, Lantern Yard, to clear up his lingering questions about the theft and the drawing of the lots. After a few days' journey, they find the old manufacturing town much changed and walk through it looking for the old chapel. The town is frightening and alien to them, with high buildings and narrow, dirty alleys. They finally reach the spot where the chapel used to be, and it is gone, having been replaced by a large factory. No one in the area knows what happened to the former residents of Lantern Yard. Silas realizes that Raveloe is his only home now, and upon his return tells Dolly that he will never know the answers to his questions. Dolly responds that it does not matter if his questions remain unanswered because that does not change the fact that he was in the right all along. Silas agrees, saying that he does not mind because he has Eppie now, and that gives him faith.

SUMMARY: CONCLUSION

Eppie and Aaron are married on a beautiful summer day. Priscilla Lammeter and her father are among those who watch the procession through the village. They have come to keep Nancy company, as Godfrey has gone away for the day "for special reasons." Priscilla tells her father that she wishes Nancy had found a child like Eppie to raise for her own. The procession stops at Mr. Macey's porch, as he is too old and frail to attend the wedding feast and has prepared some kind words for Silas. At the Rainbow, the assembling guests talk about Silas's strange story, and everyone, even the farrier, agrees that he deserves his good fortune. The wedding procession of Silas, Eppie, Aaron, and Dolly approaches the cottage. Eppie and Aaron have decided they would rather stay in Silas's cottage than go to any new home, so the cottage has been altered to accommodate Aaron. Among other improvements, a large and impressive garden has been built at Godfrey's expense. Returning home with the wedding party, Eppie tells Silas that she thinks "nobody could be happier than we are."

ANALYSIS: CHAPTERS 19–21, CONCLUSION

The final intersection of the two narrative lines resolves the novel's remaining tensions. The confrontation between Silas and the Casses over their claims to Eppie is partly a conflict of class. Despite their good intentions for Eppie's welfare, Godfrey and Nancy do not understand the depth of Silas's feelings for his daughter. Godfrey simply assumes that "deep affections can hardly go along with callous palms and scant means." Though Nancy is more sympathetic to Silas's bond with Eppie, she still regards the prospect of Eppie's belatedly restored birthright as an "unquestionable good." Also, Nancy's "code" gives precedence to the claim of the blood father over the adoptive father. Against these claims, however, Silas and Eppie's simple assertion of family easily wins out. The Casses' assumptions of upper-class superiority and the importance of blood relations are no match for Silas's simple emotion and moral certitude. Eliot here shows that Silas's "rude mind," which she describes with some condescension earlier in the novel, in fact possesses a great deal of natural nobility.

While Godfrey's attempt to make up for his past inaction is an important event, to some extent it has been predetermined by what has come before. As Silas says, after so many years, it is impossible for Godfrey to make up for his previous refusal to claim Eppie. Godfrey comes to understand that his wish to "pass for childless" when courting Nancy now means that he must continue to be childless, even though his wish has changed. Godfrey has no more managed to escape the consequences of his actions than Dunsey has. The sense of predetermination that haunts Godfrey is integral to the highly moral nature of Eliot's narrative universe. Good deeds are ultimately rewarded, and evil deeds—or cowardly inaction—are punished.

When Silas and Eppie visit Lantern Yard, they find that it is the opposite of Raveloe in more than one sense. Silas finds it a frightening and unrecognizable place. The chapel and graveyard have completely disappeared, and no one in the town remembers anything about the way things once were. Unlike Raveloe, where nothing ever goes away, in the larger town we see that people and places can disappear without a trace. The same thirty years that have utterly effaced Lantern Yard have brought virtually no comparable change to the landscape of Raveloe. The transitory nature of the larger town is partly a function of its size, but is also tied to industrialization. A factory, after all, replaces Lantern Yard's chapel. The tall buildings that Silas and Eppie pass on their way through the town, with their "gloomy" doorways filled with "sallow, begrimed" faces, contrast with the rural, outdoorsy life of Raveloe. The industrial landscape of the larger town—frightening, destructive, and dehumanizing—has wiped out memory and history.

Silas Marner closes with a final public event, bringing together all of its characters in the same way the Rainbow and the Squire's dance do. However, whereas Silas is an intruder at the public gatherings earlier in the novel, this time he is at the center. Moreover, Godfrey, who was the beau of the New Year's dance, chooses not to attend the wedding, making himself the outsider. Importantly, both Mr. Macey's statement and the wedding guests' conversations concern not the newlyweds but Silas himself. This provides yet another sign that Silas has completed his progression from the margins of the community to the center.

IMPORTANT QUOTATIONS EXPLAINED

1. To have sought a medical explanation for this
    phenomenon would have been held by Silas himself,
    as well as by his minister and fellow-members, a
    willful self-exclusion from the spiritual significance
    that might lie therein.

This passage, from Chapter 1, describes the reaction of Silas's religious sect in Lantern Yard to one of his cataleptic fits. The worshippers in his chapel interpret Silas's fit as divinely inspired, a sort of holy trance, and their respect for him grows as a result. The passage addresses the issue of faith, one of the central themes of the novel. The description suggests that the sect members' faith in the "spiritual significance" of Silas's fit requires a denial of any factors that might complicate it. In other words, the beliefs predominant in Lantern Yard do not allow for complexity or ambiguity and require that one develop intellectual blinders.

Eliot does not hesitate, in this chapter and elsewhere, to label this sort of belief primitive. There is a note of condescension in Eliot's description, a wink, shared with her contemporary readers, at these simple folk from the past who ascribe supernatural causes to anything the least bit unusual. The humor lies in the phrase "willful self-exclusion," which, Eliot implies, is exactly what Silas and his fellow worshippers depend upon to maintain their belief. It is important to keep in mind that Eliot writes as someone who had once believed quite passionately in similar teachings but had since broken from them. Thus, her view of the sect is that of someone who has both experienced and rejected similar comforts and tenets.

QUOTATIONS

2. Strangely Marner's face and figure shrank and bent themselves into a constant mechanical relation to the objects of his life, so that he produced the same sort of impression as a handle or a crooked tube, which has no meaning standing apart. The prominent eyes that used to look trusting and dreamy, now looked as if they had been made to see only one kind of thing that was very small, like tiny grain, for which they hunted everywhere; and he was so withered and yellow, that, though he was not yet forty, the children always called him "Old Master Marner."

From Chapter 2, this passage creates in Silas a portrait of the dehumanizing effects of commodified labor that Karl Marx had written about a few years prior to the publication of this novel. Silas's mechanical way of life and his worship of money make him into an almost grotesque parody of what Marx dubbed "the commodification of labor." In this way Silas serves as a harbinger of industrialization for sleepy Raveloe. For Marx, industrialization inevitably leads to a dehumanization of labor, as workers are reduced to nothing more than the amount of money that their labor is worth. Workers' social positions and ties to particular places are eliminated to create a vast, mobile labor force. In this passage, Silas is described as similarly disconnected, his humanity degraded to the status of a mere machine. He is prematurely aged, "withered and yellow," and has shrunk and bent to fit to his loom—so much so that he looks like a part of the loom, "a handle or a crooked tube, which has no meaning standing apart."

We learn that even Silas's eyesight has been damaged by his constant work. His inability to see things that are far away, is a handicap that takes on metaphorical overtones in this passage. His ability to see only "one kind of thing that was very small, for which [his eyes] hunted everywhere" shows the money-obsessed narrow-mindedness into which Silas has fallen. At this point in the novel, Silas can see only one kind of thing, gold, in everything he does. His money is the only thing that gives meaning to his life. Here, as elsewhere, Silas's physical deterioration parallels a spiritual one. Later, after Eppie brings Silas back into the community, we see another description of his eyes and learn that by then they "seem to have gathered a longer vision."

3.   This strangely novel situation of opening his trouble
to his Raveloe neighbours, of sitting in the warmth of
a hearth not his own, and feeling the presence of faces
and voices which were his nearest promise of help,
had doubtless its influence on Marner, in spite of his
passionate preoccupation with his loss. Our
consciousness rarely registers the beginning of a
growth within us any more than without us: there
have been many circulations of the sap before we
detect the smallest sign of the bud.

Here, in Chapter 7, is the first moment since his banishment from
Lantern Yard that Silas is in any way part of a community. He is at
the Rainbow, having gone there to seek help after he is robbed. The
tavern-goers sit Silas down by the hearth and make him tell his story
from beginning to end. As he does so, unbeknownst even to him,
Silas begins to experience the first stirrings of a sense of solidarity
with his neighbors. Everything about the experience is "strangely
novel" for Silas: he has never been to the Rainbow and has not in a
very long time been inside anyone's house but his own. More important, he has not in fifteen years had the experience of feeling reas-
sured by the presence of others.

    In describing these beginnings of a change, Eliot relies, as she
often does, on a metaphor drawn from the natural world. Here,
Silas is compared to a budding plant in the late winter, when the sap
has started to circulate but before there is any outward sign of life.
This image of rebirth suggests an idea of community as something
natural and organic, as opposed to the unnatural, deforming isolation from which Silas is beginning to emerge.

4.   Godfrey was silent. He was not likely to be very
       penetrating in his judgments, but he had always had a
       sense that his father's indulgence had not been
       kindness, and had had a vague longing for some
       discipline that would have checked his own errant
       weakness and helped his better will.

Here, in Chapter 9, Godfrey is weathering a severe tongue-lashing from his father, Squire Cass, after confessing that he lent Dunsey rent money from one of his father's tenants. The Squire complains that he has been "too good a father" and has spoiled his sons. In this regard, the Cass household provides a counterpoint to the domestic life Silas and Eppie later create. Both Godfrey and Eppie grow up motherless—the former in circumstances of great plenty, the latter with little. Both fathers indulge their children, but while the Squire does so out of negligence, Silas does so out of love. Eppie never doubts Silas's love for her, whereas Godfrey, in this passage, has precisely that doubt about his father. Eliot implies that this crucial difference is the reason Godfrey has grown up weak-willed and cowardly, while Eppie possesses a strong sense of values. This contrast is all the more striking since Eppie is in fact Godfrey's natural daughter.

The passage also highlights the perspective that Eliot's narrator takes throughout the novel. This omniscient narrator is not constrained simply to report what is seen and heard. Here, we go inside Godfrey's head and have access to ideas that he thinks but does not express aloud. The narrator takes this even one step further, not only divulging what Godfrey is thinking, but passing judgment on Godfrey's general intelligence. At the same time, however, judging from the Squire's behavior, the conclusion at which Godfrey gropingly arrives is correct. This sort of narration—omniscient, judgmental, but ultimately sympathetic toward the characters—is an important characteristic not only of this novel, but of all of Eliot's works.

5.   I can't say what I should have done about that,
       Godfrey. I should never have married anybody else.
       But I wasn't worth doing wrong for—nothing is in
       this world. Nothing is so good as it seems
       beforehand—not even our marrying wasn't, you see.

Nancy gently upbraids Godfrey with these lines in Chapter 18, after
he confesses that he is Eppie's father and has hidden that fact from
Nancy for eighteen years. Nancy's reaction is not one of anger, but
instead one of deep regret that Godfrey had not claimed Eppie long
ago, so they could have raised her themselves. When Godfrey
responds that Nancy would never have married him had she known
of his secret child, she responds with these lines, a gentle condemna-
tion of Godfrey's act and the thinking that justified it.

The quote brings Nancy's "unalterable little code" of behavior
into confrontation with Godfrey's slippery, self-justifying equivoca-
tion. While Nancy and her code are portrayed as occasionally arbitrary and even illogical, Eliot leaves no doubt that Nancy is a deeply
moral person. In taking Godfrey to task for simply molding his
actions to contingency, Nancy is passing Eliot's judgment, as well.
Here, as elsewhere, Eliot's narrative punishes those who, by allow-
ing ends to justify means, ignore basic questions of right and wrong.

QUOTATIONS

KEY FACTS

FULL TITLE
Silas Marner: The Weaver of Raveloe

AUTHOR
George Eliot

TYPE OF WORK
Novel

GENRE
Victorian novel, novel of manners, pastoral fiction

LANGUAGE
English

TIME AND PLACE WRITTEN
1860–61, London

DATE OF FIRST PUBLICATION
1861

PUBLISHER
William Blackwood and Sons

NARRATOR
An anonymous omniscient speaker with no part in the plot

POINT OF VIEW
The narrator speaks in the omniscient third person, describing what the characters are seeing, feeling, and thinking and what they are failing to see, feel, and think. The narrator uses the first person singular "I," but at no point enters the story as a character. Near the beginning, a personal story unrelated to the action of the novel is relayed to provide corroborating evidence for a generalization, hinting that the narrator is a real person.

TONE
Morally uncompromising, slightly condescending, but nevertheless deeply sympathetic to characters' failings

TENSE
Past

SETTING (TIME)
The "early years" of the nineteenth century

SETTING (PLACE)
Raveloe, a fictional village in the English countryside

PROTAGONIST
Silas Marner

MAJOR CONFLICT
Silas Marner lives for a long time without any connection to other human beings or his youthful faith in God. Though he does not struggle to find purpose and connection in his life, the novel is about his recovery of purpose, faith, and community through his finding Eppie.

RISING ACTION
Silas spends fifteen years in relative isolation, amassing a hoard of gold coins that is then stolen by Dunstan Cass.

CLIMAX
Eppie appears in Silas's cottage, and he decides to adopt her.

FALLING ACTION
When Godfrey fails to claim Eppie as his daughter and marries Nancy, Silas raises Eppie. Silas's love and care for Eppie make him a revered member of the Raveloe community, ending his isolation. Sixteen years later, Godfrey admits that he is Eppie's father and tries to adopt her, but she elects to stay with Silas.

THEMES
The individual versus the community; character as destiny; the interdependence of faith and community

MOTIFS
The natural world; domesticity; class

SYMBOLS
Silas's loom; Lantern Yard; the hearth

FORESHADOWING
Silas opening his door to look outside as Eppie toddles toward his cottage; Mr. Macey telling Silas his money will be returned to him; Dunsey claiming that he always lands on his feet.

STUDY QUESTIONS & ESSAY TOPICS

STUDY QUESTIONS

1. *What is the significance of Silas Marner's nearsightedness?*

Silas's poor eyesight is part of the bodily deterioration and deformation he has experienced as the result of his long hours of work at the loom. Like his bent frame and premature aging, it is a mark of the dehumanizing qualities of long, repetitive labor. On the level of plot development, Silas's poor vision creates a parallel between Eppie and Silas's lost gold. He does not see Eppie come in, just as he did not see the gold leave. When he first notices Eppie, Silas sees her blonde hair and thinks that somehow his gold has returned. He must touch her hair in order to understand that Eppie is a living thing. On a symbolic level, Silas's nearsightedness embodies his general narrowness of vision and thought—a limitation that, until Eppie comes into his life, prevents him from thinking beyond the narrow confines of his work and his gold. It is significant that, when we see Silas sixteen years after he has adopted Eppie and grown out of his spiritual straitjacket, his eyes "seem to have gathered a longer vision, as is the way with eyes that have been shortsighted in early life."

2.   *Compare Silas Marner's love of his money to his*
       religious faith.

For fifteen years, Silas's gold serves as a substitute for his lost faith. Silas loves his gold, works for it, and looks forward to viewing it and holding it in his hands each evening. He even comes to love the faces engraved on the coins as if they were his friends. But, as is made clear when Eppie appears, in his miserliness Silas has wasted his love on something that has no capacity to reciprocate. Unlike his lost faith, Silas's love of his money is simply a desire and does not involve any higher system of beliefs. Moreover, Silas's love of his money could be seen as the *opposite* of faith in that it renders his actions important only as a means to obtain more gold. Conversely, a life of faith, as exemplified by Dolly Winthrop, is one in which actions have meaning as manifestations of belief.

The other major difference is that religious faith is a communal experience. In both Lantern Yard and Raveloe, community is formed around shared faith. According to Dolly's simple theology, religious faith is intimately associated with a faith in one's neighbors, and the church is seen as responsible for those members of the community who cannot care for themselves. Silas's guineas, on the other hand, draw him away from the world and shut him up in the isolation of his cottage.

3.   *What does Silas Marner's cottage represent?*

Silas's stone cottage functions as a symbol of domesticity, one of Eliot's primary motifs in the novel. Silas's is a strange sort of domesticity, since the cottage is hardly furnished, but the cottage is still very much Silas's private space. For Silas to be incorporated into the community, he must first be drawn out from his isolation in the cottage. Thus, the novel's two most important events are intrusions into Silas's cottage, first by Dunsey and then by Eppie. After each intrusion, Silas is forced to leave the cottage to seek help in the public space of the village.

Similarly, the cottage functions as a marker of Silas's growth into the community. Initially, when Silas is isolated and without faith, his home is bleak and closed off from the outside world, with its doors tightly shut. As Silas begins to open himself up, his cottage likewise opens up. As Silas and Eppie become a family, the home is literally brightened and filled with new life, as the family gets several animals and improves the garden and yard.

The Cass household, the Red House, functions as a counterpoint to Silas's cottage. While at the opposite extreme of size and luxury from Silas's abode, the Cass home also undergoes a transformation as it moves from the Squire's control to Nancy's. The Red House plays host to two major social events in the novel: the New Year's dance and Aaron and Eppie's wedding procession. However, while Silas's home continues to grow and take on new members, the Red House becomes increasingly subdued and has fewer occupants at the novel's close than at its beginning.

QUESTIONS & ESSAYS

SUGGESTED ESSAY TOPICS

1. Is there a difference between superstition and religion in the novel? If so, what is the difference?

2. Discuss the importance of labor in the novel.

3. How does social class function in the novel?

4. Why does Silas wish to visit Lantern Yard again? What does his visit accomplish?

5. Compare Nancy's and Dolly's systems of belief.

6. Eliot sets her novel in the recent, but nonetheless irretrievable, past. In what ways does she foreshadow the end of the world she describes?

7. The novel is set up as two parallel narratives that intersect three times. How do these meetings show a progression in Silas's status as a member of the community?

8. Discuss the significance of the novel's epigraph.

Review & Resources

Quiz

1. Why are weavers typically objects of suspicion in Silas's day?

    A.   They are seen as doing womanly work
    B.   They are rootless and have specialized knowledge
    C.   They wear only linen clothing
    D.   They have bad eyesight

2. How does Silas know about herbal medicine?

    A.   His mother taught him
    B.   It was part of the training from his religious sect in Lantern Yard
    C.   He has read up on the topic
    D.   He doesn't, he only pretends to

3. What is dropsy?

    A.   A part of a loom
    B.   A traditional British breakfast drink
    C.   The name of Silas's pet bunny rabbit
    D.   A disease that causes abnormal swelling in the body

4. Why doesn't Silas protest his innocence when he is framed for theft?

    A.   He is not allowed to speak
    B.   He is having a cataleptic fit at the time
    C.   He believes God will clear him
    D.   He believes he actually did steal the money while having a cataleptic fit

5. During the period in his life when all he does is work and hoard money, Silas is likened to:

    A.   A spider
    B.   A narrow, nearly dried-up rivulet
    C.   A handle or crooked tube
    D.   All of the above

6. From where does Godfrey obtain the one hundred pounds that he lends Dunsey?

    A.   The sale of Godfrey's horse, Wildfire
    B.   The rent paid by one of the Squire's tenants
    C.   Money that Godfrey had set aside to give his wife, Molly
    D.   Godfrey's winnings at cards

7. Why does Godfrey put up with Dunsey's bullying?

    A.   Dunsey can beat him up
    B.   Dunsey has threatened to expose Godfrey's secret marriage
    C.   Godfrey is trying to set an example of good Christian forbearance
    D.   Godfrey is a masochist and enjoys abuse

8. Why does Dunsey almost turn around and return home before he gets to the hunt?

    A.   He thinks of the idea of bullying Silas into lending money to Godfrey
    B.   He wants Godfrey to have to admit to the Squire where the missing money went
    C.   He has forgotten his riding whip
    D.   He gets cold feet

9. Where does Silas go when he finds his gold missing?

    A.   The church
    B.   Dolly Winthrop's house
    C.   The Rainbow
    D.   The Red House

10. What is a farrier?

    A. A species of large fox

    B. A rank of cavalry officer

    C. Someone who shoes horses and generally tends to livestock diseases

    D. A knot used to tie off a piece of linen

11. To whom does everyone in town suspect the mysterious tinder-box belongs?

    A. Silas

    B. Jem Rodney

    C. The peddler

    D. Mr. Lammeter

12. What do Mr. Crackenthorp, Mr. Macey, and Dolly Winthrop all suggest when they come to visit Silas after he loses his money?

    A. That he take up a collection

    B. That he lock his door

    C. That he go to church

    D. That he adopt a child

13. Why does Nancy arrive at the New Year's dance resolved to reject Godfrey?

    A. Her father does not approve of him

    B. She finds him lacking in character

    C. He has mocked her strict code of behavior

    D. He has been too forward with her

14. Why is Molly Farren coming to the New Year's dance?

    A. She wants to announce her and Godfrey's marriage to everyone there

    B. She thinks she can win Godfrey's love by dancing with him

    C. She wants to apologize to Godfrey for something she has said

    D. She wants her daughter to be adopted by Godfrey and Nancy

REVIEW & RESOURCES

15. Why do Nancy and Priscilla wear the same dress to the New Year's dance?

    A. Because Priscilla wants to look like Nancy
    B. Because they are going to perform a duet
    C. It is purely by accident
    D. Because Nancy insists that sisters should dress identically

16. How is Eppie able to enter Silas's cottage so easily?

    A. Silas is out on an errand and has left the door open
    B. The door is locked, but she climbs through the window
    C. Silas is holding the door open and is in the midst of one of his fits
    D. She comes in the back door, which has no lock

17. What is Silas's first thought when he notices that the mass of gold on his hearth is in fact a baby girl?

    A. That he should lock his door
    B. That he will adopt the little girl
    C. That the little girl's mother can't be far away
    D. That the little girl is his dead sister, coming back to him in a dream

18. What does Silas attempt to do to discipline Eppie?

    A. Read her long passages from the Bible
    B. Spank her
    C. Tie her to the loom
    D. Put her in the coal-hole

19. Why doesn't Godfrey go by the title of Squire?

    A. His father's property was divided up at his death and therefore Godfrey did not inherit the title
    B. He finds it pretentious
    C. Squire was actually his father's first name
    D. Nancy cannot pronounce it

20. What is Godfrey's role in Eppie's life?

   A. He takes her on walks
   B. He helps pay for things and donates furniture
   C. He reads her bedtime stories
   D. He tells her about her mother

21. Why does Nancy refuse for so long to adopt Eppie?

   A. She dislikes children
   B. She thinks Godfrey will love Eppie more than he
      loves her
   C. She thinks it is wrong for Godfrey and her to have
      something that fate has denied them
   D. She suspects that Eppie is Godfrey's child and wants
      him to be punished

22. What prompts Godfrey to confess his secret?

   A. He finds out that he is terminally ill
   B. Dunsey's remains are discovered in the drained
      stone-pit
   C. He gets drunk
   D. All of the above

23. When Godfrey confesses to Eppie that he is her father, what
    is her reaction?

   A. She is repulsed by him and has no desire to leave Silas
      for him
   B. She is tempted by the life he offers but decides to stay
      with Silas nonetheless
   C. She is angry with him, primarily for having
      abandoned her mother
   D. She sympathizes with Nancy for having married such
      a coward

24. Why does Silas decide to return to Lantern Yard for a visit?

    A. He is looking for work
    B. He wants to find out if he was ever cleared of theft, and to ask his old minister about the drawing of the lots
    C. He wants Eppie to see where he grew up
    D. He wants to show his former sect that he has succeeded in spite of his excommunication

25. What is Nancy's reaction to Godfrey's confession that he had a previous marriage and child?

    A. She leaves him for Dunsey
    B. She pretends not to hear him
    C. She expresses regret that he didn't tell her sooner, so they could have adopted Eppie
    D. She says that she would never have married him if she had known

REVIEW & RESOURCES

ANSWER KEY:
1: B; 2: A; 3: D; 4: C; 5: D; 6: B; 7: B; 8: A; 9: C; 10: C;
11: C; 12: C; 13: B; 14: A; 15: D; 16: C; 17: D; 18: D; 19: A;
20: B; 21: C; 22: B; 23: A; 24: B; 25: C

SUGGESTIONS FOR FURTHER READING

ASHTON, ROSEMARY. *George Eliot: A Life.* New York: Allen Lane / The Penguin Press, 1996.

BEER, JOHN B. *Providence and Love: Studies in Wordsworth, Channing, Myers, George Eliot, and Ruskin.* New York: Oxford University Press, 1998.

BODENHEIMER, ROSEMARIE. *The Real Life of Mary Ann Evans: George Eliot, Her Letters and Fiction.* Ithaca, New York: Cornell University Press, 1994.

CARROLL, DAVID, ed. *George Eliot: The Critical Heritage.* London: Routledge, 1995.

HARDY, BARBARA NATHAN, ed. *Critical Essays on George Eliot.* London: Routledge & K. Paul, 1970.

HUTCHINSON, STUART, ed. *George Eliot: Critical Assessments.* Robertsbridge, UK: Helm Information, 1996.

LEVINE, GEORGE, ed. *The Cambridge Companion to George Eliot.* New York: Cambridge University Press, 2001.

SHOWALTER, ELAINE. *A Literature of Their Own: British Women Novelists from Bronte to Lessing.* Princeton, New Jersey: Princeton University Press, 1999.

REVIEW & RESOURCES

SPARKNOTES STUDY GUIDES: